Where Rivers Meet

The Story of
Dr. S. F. Monestime
Canada's First Black Mayor

Doug Mackey

Past Forward
Heritage Limited

Published by Past Forward Heritage Limited
330 Sumach Street #41, Toronto, ON M5A 3K7
(416) 925-8412, www.pastforward.ca

Library and Archives Canada Cataloguing in Publication

Mackey, Doug, 1931-
    Where rivers meet : the story of Dr. S.F. Monestime, Canada's first Black mayor / Doug Mackey.

ISBN 978-1-896974-08-8

    1. Monestime, S. F. (S. Firmin), 1909-1977. 2. Mayors--Ontario--Mattawa--Biography. 3. Black Canadians--Biography. 4. Haitian Canadians--Biography.
5. Physicians--Ontario--Mattawa--Biography. 6. Physicians--Haiti--Biography.
7. Monestime, Zena. 8. Mattawa (Ont.)--Biography. 9. Mattawa (Ont.)--History.
I. Title.

FC3099.M384Z49 2009   971.3'14704092   C2009-901231-6

Book editing and design by Paul Mackey.

Front Cover Photograph: Dr. Monestime stands at the head of Mattawa's Main Street where the Trans-Canada Highway passes through Mattawa. The first building on the left is the Trans-Canada Hotel and the second is the former location of the Chez Francois Restaurant. The Trans-Canada burned down and the restaurant is gone. Both buildings play an important part in this story. The bridge over the Mattawa River is in the background of the photo. The maps are of Mattawa, Gdansk on the Baltic Sea and Haiti.

Back Cover Photograph: The photo of the Monestime family was taken by *North Bay Nugget* photographer Bud Berry in 1969 and shows Dr. Monestime, his wife Zena, daughter Vala and son Fedia. Sons Sasha and Yura are in front with Zena's mother Valentina (Babie) in the back. The Dr. Monestime for President badge was used by his supporters when he ran unsuccessfully for the Presidency of the Progressive Conservative Party of Canada in 1971.

Photograph Credits: (MDM) Mattawa & District Museum, (LM) Life Magazine, (NHB) Natural Heritage Books, (EE) Ed Eng Photography, (BE) Bob Emond. Medical bag shown on title page is from the Dr. S. F. Monestime exhibit in the Mattawa & District Museum.

Mattawa

There is a story here where rivers meet,
Too noble for the vehicle of rhyme,
A tale of searching eyes, intrepid feet,
A tale whose telling mocks the hand of time.
I stand where once the dauntless Champlain stood
And scan the foothills on the neighbouring shore,
I sense the awe inspiring solitude
And feel a peace I've never felt before.
This cradle of the north once rocked a dream,
And nursed a breed that made the dream come true.
O conquerors of forest, hill and stream,
How shall a poem mark a grave for you!
No! Let these meeting rivers be your shrine:
Yours is the deed…the heritage is mine.

Len G. Selle - Mattawa poet circa 1950s

I have a dream that my four little children will one day live in a nation where they will not be judged by the color of their skin, but by the content of their character.

Dr. Martin Luther King Jr. - Lincoln Memorial, Washington, DC 1963

A man whose father less than 60 years ago might not have been served at a local restaurant can now stand before you to take a most sacred oath.

U. S. President Barak Obama - Inauguration speech, 2009

The memory of the man would not easily be forgotten and wherever the townspeople of Mattawa should meet, Firmin Monestime would always be a popular and welcome subject of conversation.

Reporter Gordon McCulloch - 1977

Introduction

The signs at the entrances to the town of Mattawa say: "There is a story here where rivers meet."* There are, of course, many stories here where the Mattawa River meets the mighty Ottawa River in the shadow of the Laurentian Highlands. This book tells the story of Dr. Saint Firmin Monestime and his family on the centenary of his birth in 1909. This is only one of the many stories that will be told about Mattawa on the 2009, 125th anniversary of Mattawa's establishment, and that make Mattawa the remarkable place it is.

The title of this book is a metaphor for the flowing together of cultures in our multicultural nation, where various peoples come together to create unique stories. In this case, two diverse and distant cultures merge with improbable and resounding results.

This story, simply told, shows that with vision, confidence, hard work and community support, remarkable things can happen that have an impact on a community's way of life. There is no question that in this story, the people of Mattawa share in the achievement by their openness, generosity and acceptance. This book is one of the ways that we celebrate a man, his family, his friends and his community one hundred years after his birth and on the 125th anniversary of the community where they flourished.

Doug Mackey 2009

*Mattawa poet Len G. Selle wrote the poem that this line comes from. See over to read the poem. To read more about Len G. Selle see Appendix 4.

Acknowledgements

Vala, Yura and Sasha Monestime conceived the idea of this book to review, honour and celebrate the lives of their parents, Firmin and Zena Monestime. As a regional historian with an affection for Mattawa, it was an honour to be asked to prepare this book. The family wanted a history of general interest with many graphics to help tell the story. It is hoped that the book will help people of all ages to know and appreciate this story of Mattawa as a positive example of multicultural and Black history.

The book would not have been written without the full cooperation of the family, including interviews, archival material and the freedom to write as I chose. It also could not have been written without the help of numerous Monestime colleagues, friends and others who shared their stories with me. The general affection and respect for the family was overwhelming. I also must thank the *North Bay Nugget* for the invaluable news reports and photographs.

Thanks to my son Paul, who has edited, designed and published all of Past Forward's books including this one and has created and maintained my Heritage Perspectives website. Thanks to Bernadette Kerr, who did the word-processing, some editing and has done so with most of my "Community Voices - Heritage Perspectives" columns for the *North Bay Nugget* for years.

Table of Contents:

Bird's-eye view of Mattawa looking south. Quebec and the Ottawa River, heading to Ottawa, are on the left. The Mattawa River enters the Ottawa River from the right.

1
Mattawa

"There is a story here where rivers meet" - Len G. Selle

IN THE SUMMER of 1951 Dr. Monestime, a recently Canadian certified MD and his colleague Dr. G. Lamontagne heard about openings for doctors in Timmins and decided to drive there from Ottawa to look the situation over. At noon on the trip, as they approached the beautiful town of Mattawa, they looked for a place to stop for lunch. As they entered Main Street, the Chez Francois restaurant caught their eye and they stopped. "I didn't intend to come here," Dr. Monestime recalled years later.

A brief history of Mattawa up to the 1950s will set the scene for this story.

Mattawa History

Mattawa is situated in the shadow of the Laurentian Highlands where the Mattawa River meets the mighty Ottawa River between Ontario and Quebec heading to the St. Lawrence.

First People

There are indications that Native people appeared here five to six thousand years ago after the last ice age 10,000 years ago. When the two to three kilometres of ice slowly receded the land rose and waterways that existed were shaped and new ones were formed. As the ice sheet withdrew it scraped and smoothed the earth's surface and vegetation eventually began to grow and wildlife began to appear. Native people, like people today, were undoubtedly drawn to the junction of the Mattawa and Ottawa Rivers for a variety of reasons but primarily because of its location as a natural gathering place for rest and business.

First Europeans

About 400 years ago the first Europeans appeared in the area led by Samuel

Mattawa in 1950 looking north. The Chez Francois Restaurant is on the left.

de Champlain. In 1610 Étienne Brûlé, one of Champlain's men, entered the unknown territory to the west and met and mingled with the Native people. In 1615 Champlain stopped here on his way to Lake Nipissing and beyond. The knowledge and experience of the Native people was critical to the success of the French and later for explorers, surveyors, priests, fur traders and eventually settlers.

Native Groups

The aboriginal connection in Mattawa was consolidated when two Algonquin bands under two chiefs migrated to the area in the early 1800s and became permanent residents. Chief Amable du Fond established his band's hunting ground south of the Mattawa River and used the river that now bears his name as his travel route. Chief Antoine Kiwiwissens had the area to the north where his name remains on Antoine Creek and Antoine Township.

Two Native groups in Mattawa currently represent their peoples' interests in a wide variety of ways and play an important role in the community. The Madajawan North Bay/Mattawa Algonquins have a wide general interest in native affairs. The Antoine First Nation has a similar interest with a primary focus on descendants of Chief Antoine. With extensive intermarriage there are many Métis people in Mattawa as well.

Fur Trade

As the lucrative fur trade developed, the monopoly of the English Hudson's Bay Company was challenged by the French along the St. Lawrence-Ottawa-Mattawa and points West fur trade route. The early independent entrepreneurs—the coureurs de bois—gathered furs from the Native population. Eventually the North West Company was formed by the French and the furs were gathered by the famous Voyageurs in their large canoes. After the British Conquest in 1763 the two companies joined and became the

A painting of the Village of Mattawa around the time of its incorporation in 1884. Lumbermens' pointer boats can be seen passing under the bridge built across the Mattawa River in the 1877. (MDM)

WHERE RIVERS MEET

Hudson's Bay Company.

A Hudson's Bay trading post, a satellite of the Temiscaming post, was built in 1837 to handle the furs & supplies in the Mattawa area.

Lumbering and Expansion

As the fur trade in the area diminished the need for lumber for shipbuilding in England and elsewhere became important. By the mid 1800s there were permanent settlers in Mattawa and several hotels and businesses catering to the lumber trade were established.

Churches and schools were built as Mattawa grew. A hospital run by the Catholic Church was begun. The Chief Amable du

This was the first car in Mattawa in 1910. The driver is Albert Gauvreau, beside him is Fred Chaput, father of John Chaput, 1950s MPP for Nipissing. (MDM)

The Murrays & Loughrin store in the 1880s when Mattawa was becoming a prosperous settlement . (MDM)

A log boom on the Mattawa River in the 1930s. On the North shore there is the St. Anne's Roman Catholic Church (centre), St. Anne's School (right) and the Mattawa General Hospital (left). This Hospital was built in 1904 to replace the one built in 1885 which burned down. In 1966 this building also burned down. (MDM)

Below: The La Cave Rapids dam, built for the Otto Holden Generating Station, under construction in early 1950s.(MDM)
Right: Some of the workers who built the dam. (MDM)

WHERE RIVERS MEET

Fond log house and a house next door opposite what is now Timmins Park served as a chapel, school and hospital for a period. A bridge was constructed across the Mattawa River to join the two parts of the village in 1877 and a railway bridge to Quebec was built in 1896.

Steamboat service to Mattawa was established as was a road along the Ottawa River. The railway which became the Canadian Pacific Railway (CPR) went through Mattawa in 1881. Hydro power became available in 1894 when the Hurdman Dam was built two kilometres west of Mattawa on the Mattawa River. Mattawa was incorporated 125 years ago as a village in 1884 and became a town in 1892.

Mattawa in 1950

At mid century Mattawa's quiet existence was energized when the Otto Holden Generating Station was built at the La Cave Rapids eight kilometres north of Mattawa on the Ottawa River. The population of the area rose by over 1000 and business boomed. The CPR's transcontinental train traveled through Mattawa four times a day and a separate Mattawa-North Bay train ran regularly. The Trans-Canada Highway (Hwy. 17) which was started in the Depression as a work project, provided a route for cars and trucks bringing business to hotels and restaurants, and gas stations.

Logging and lumbering was the main business with several supporting operations. The

The owner of the Chez Francois restaurant, Francois Martin, in his office. Behind him is his wife Lina. In the late 1940s Francois had been to Ottawa for an operation.

Guelph Cask Veneer Company, Fred Lafreniere Lumber, Weyerhauser, G.W. Martin, and Sklar were well known operations. The Duval Lumber Company came to Snake Creek in 1959 and eventually moved to Highway 17 west of Mattawa.

A high school was built in 1945 and a movie theatre in 1949. In 1957 Highway 533 to Temiscaming, Quebec was completed. Mattawa's population had grown over the years with 1,462 people in 1921, 1,613 in 1931, 1,971 in 1941 and 3,097 in 1951.

Doctor Shortage

In 1951 Dr. J.A. Bergeron, one of Mattawa's two doctors, died after 27 years of service. The records show that at least three doctors visited briefly as a possible replacement—none stayed.

The story of what happened

next when our two doctors driving from Ottawa entered the Chez Francois restaurant on Mattawa's Main Street is local legend. Dr. Saint Firmin Monestime, a Black doctor from the Caribbean nation of Haiti, later recalled: "When I sat down I saw the manager look at me in surprise and I thought he didn't want me in his restaurant. This part of the country wasn't too familiar with negroes."

Dr. Monestime's experiences with prejudice in his home country of Haiti and in the U.S. had made him unsure of what reception he would receive in Northern Ontario.

Saint Firmin Monestime, MD

2
Haiti to Canada

"Having witnessed countless scenes of misery, we wanted to intelligently help those looking to shine a little light into the homes of our countrymen."- Dr. Monestime's introduction to his book on rural medicine in Haiti, 1940

A HUNDRED YEARS AGO, on December 16th, 1909 Saint Firmin Monestime was born in Cape Haitian, Haiti, to Monsieur et Madame Saint Germain Monestime. He was the only son in a family of seven children and, as was the custom in Haiti, the male child was given special status. His father was a successful tanner and could afford a good education for his son who turned out to be intelligent, hard working, ambitious, and capable.

U.S. Occupation

Firmin, or "tit saint" as he was called by family and friends, grew up during the United States occupation of Haiti which lasted from 1916 until 1935. (For more on Haitian history see Appendix 1.) One of his early memories was of a photograph of the body of Haitian leader and hero General Charlemagne Peralte, who lead the revolt against the U.S. occupation, crucified on a barn door. The photo was circulated by the U.S. forces to intimidate the population. He recalled: "there was martial law and you couldn't have a light on after ten o'clock at night. It does not say much for the Americans but under those conditions I became allergic to English and would not learn it."

Firmin received his early education from age seven to nineteen at the Lyceum in Port au Prince. He attended University and graduated with a B. A. degree in 1931 at age 22. He taught history

National Palace of Haiti, Port-au-Prince 1937. (LM)

briefly. He then attended the University Of Haiti Medical School graduating with a medical degree.

Genocide

After completing his studies, he was named Medical Officer on the International Route between Haiti, a former French colony, and the former Spanish colony the Dominican Republic. He recalled traveling by donkey, often crossing over rivers on suspension bridges or on "mountainous roads skirting cliff faces" through this wild area made up of mountains, valleys, and rivers.

He was on duty in October 1937 when Dominican Republic President Raphael Trujillo ordered the genocide of Haitians who were living in the disputed area in the Dominican Republic.

Twenty to thirty thousand Haitians were killed, many only because they spoke French or Creole instead of Spanish. "I saw all kinds of broken bodies. I helped bury the dead. There, I

Photograph of the body of Haitian rebel leader and hero General Charlemagne Peralte.

realized that, in death, as it should be in life, there is no difference between coloured and white people," Dr. Monestime recalled.

Once Dr. Monestime was mistakenly arrested by Haitian soldiers but was released the next day. He also recalled that the Red Cross waited three months before bringing in medical supplies.

For his contribution he received the *Chevalier de l'Ordre*

National Honneur et Mérite.

Dr. Monestime became Director of the Department of Rural Medicine in the Capital, Port au Prince, establishing an excellent reputation. He began to write about rural medicine and eventually wrote four books, *L'Alimentation du paysan, L'Agriculture et la Médecine rurale en Haiti, 2ème. Série de conférences de médecine rurale* and *Conférences de médecine rurale* (see sidebar page 16).

During this period he married Nelly Bonhomme and had two children, Daniel and Eddie, before dissolving the marriage.

Political Troubles

During this time politics in Haiti was difficult and he began to speak out, write and go on the radio to express his views on the "deplorable conditions" in Haiti. He included influential families in his attacks.

In frustration over the politics of Haiti he resigned his position and sought a different

This photograph from Life Magazine in 1937 shows refugees from the genocide receiving food at Ouanaminthe Village Hall. Many of these people's relatives were killed. (LM)

Young survivor of the massacre. Perhaps his wounds were treated by Dr. Monestime. (LM)

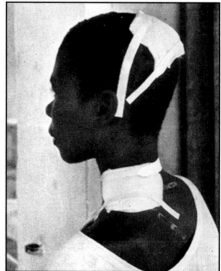

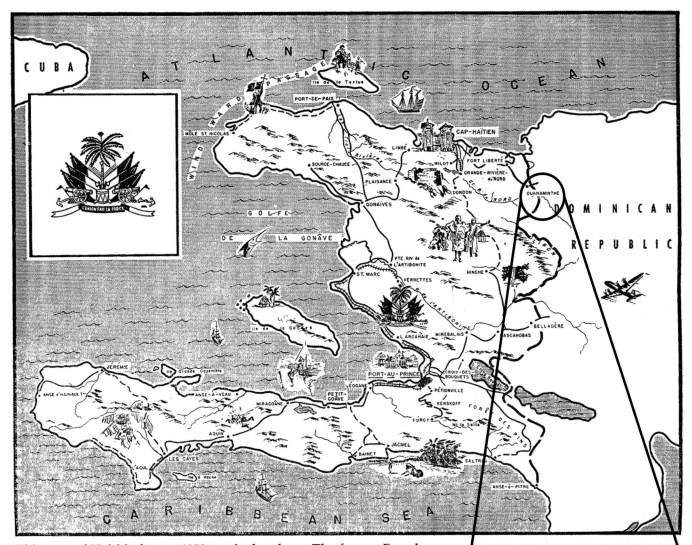

This map of Haiti is from a 1952 tourist brochure. The former French colony of Haiti is a mountainous nation that occupies the western third of the island of Hispaniola which it shares with the former Spanish colony the Dominican Republic. Circled is the location of the 1937 genocide of Haitians by Dominican Republic troops. (MDM)

future. His status was compromised by leaving the government service. He said: "In Haiti you become an enemy of the state as soon as you leave the civil service. I was afraid for my life."

Technically he was not to leave the country. He considered going to the U.S. but was concerned by the racism there. He had never learned English as a reaction to the American presence in Haiti so speaking only the French language was a prob-

lem. He considered France but there were too many problems there after the chaos of the Second World War.

He found an opening in Quebec where his skills were appreciated. He left Haiti "quietly," without announcing his departure, for fear of reprisals.

On his way to Quebec his plane landed in Miami, Florida. When he got off the plane and headed to the washroom he was faced with a choice of two washroom doors one for "whites" and

The river on the border between the Dominican Republic and Haiti. Many Haitian settlers on the Dominican side of the river (right) were killed because they did not speak spanish. (LM)

Introduction to Book on Rural Medicine

The following is an abridged copy in English of the introduction Dr. Monestime made to *Conférences de médicine rurale*. The book was produced as a follow up to courses taught to Haitian teachers in August 1940. It shows his early leadership, and courage in criticizing government policies that eventually got him in trouble with the country's leaders.

He states: "the time has come to show the country's current leaders what we have done for rural Haitian farmers recently abandoned to servitude and ignorance." He goes on to say: "The primary illnesses that dominate in Haiti's rural areas are malaria, yaws, syphilis and intestinal parasites. These illnesses hinder farming activities, sap the enthusiasm of school children and, in our view, are a national scourge.

Having witnessed countless scenes of misery, we wanted to intelligently help those looking to shine a little light into the homes of our countrymen. Any work done on their behalf must be based on improving their health."

He praised the "Rural Education teachers who, in doing their job, pay no heed to the fatigue or emotion that comes with the mountainous roads skirting cliff faces."

He went on to say: "To all our friends who have helped us present

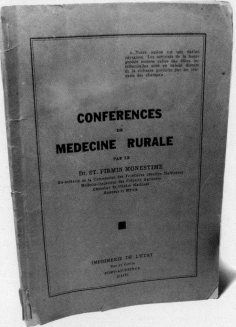

these concepts of rural medicine to the public, we owe our deepest gratitude.

To our parents, children, and brothers and sisters on the frontier, we also dedicate these pages, which represent the beginning of our struggle to combat the illnesses affecting the inhabitants of our countryside. We cannot cast aside our close bonds of kinship that come from our very origin. In closing, we thank all those who spontaneously made this modest work possible.-Dr. S. F. Monestime, August, 1940."

Dr. Monestime did not have a copy of his book until a friend, Haitian historian and author Laurore St.Juste, provided him with a copy in 1970 when St.Juste was in New York. Correspondence indicates that he had a copy of the "important and precious book" for Dr. Monestime and would forward it to him. Receiving it undoubtedly brought pleasure to Dr. Monestime, bringing back memories of times past and allowing us to share his achievement here.

The swearing in ceremony of General Paul Eugene Magloire as President of Haiti in 1950. The postcard was sent to Dr. Monestime by Haitian historian Laurore St Juste. Laurore wrote: "My Dear Monestime, in the words of the great Napoleon, a picture is worth a thousand words. That is why, instead of boring you with endless pages, I am sending you this postcard to give you an idea of the colossal demonstration that was the swearing-in of our President. Old Tiger, I wish you a happy and healthy New Year. Laurore." Dr. Monestime was offered a position as professor in Haiti but he chose to stay in Canada.

Dr. Saint Firmin Monestime posing with fellow students in Canada.

the other for "colored." "I was so insulted," he recalled. When he went to buy his ticket to Canada he also had to stand in a separate line for "colored" people.

Canada

On July 26, 1945 Dr. Monestime arrived in Quebec with a dollar in his pocket. "I took a taxi to Enfant Jesus Hospital. The charge was 90 cents and I gave the driver a 10-cent tip," he recalled. "After what I had seen, I was surprised at my reception in Canada. The people were wonderful and I was very happy."

He was one of the first of a very small group of Haitian professionals who came to Quebec in the 1940s. During the 1950s and 1960s thousands of Haitian exiled immigrants came to Canada.

Dr. Monestime had to take training and had to intern for several years to get his full Canadian medical accreditation. He spent the better part of a year in Quebec City developing his specialization in gynecology. He then became a Senior Intern in Gynecology in Quebec City and in General Surgery in Verdun Quebec. He was later the Assistant to the Head of Obstetrics and Gynecology, Dr. Burke Ewing, at the Ottawa General Hospital where he tutored other interns.

On graduation he became one of the first, if not the first, Haitian medical doctors licensed in Canada. In 1950 Dr. Monestime was offered a position as professor in Haiti but he chose to stay in Canada. He was ready to start a new life.

As mentioned Dr. Monestime had been married in Haiti before coming to Canada. During his years of training in Canada he did not develop a lasting personal relationship.

In 1950 he was invited to a Christmas party. Also invited were Valentina Petschersky and her attractive daughter Zinaida. They were Russian refugees, or "displaced persons" as they were called at the time, from the Second World War.

Zinaida (Zena) Petschersky

3
Russia to Canada

"We have forgotten what peace feels like. We no longer know how to laugh. Every thought, every conversation revolves around the war." - Zena Petschersky 1943.

ZINAIDA'S FATHER Feodor Alexandrovitch Petschersky fled from the Russian Revolution in 1917. He relocated to the free city of Danzig (now Gdansk) in the Polish Corridor that was established by the Treaty of Versailles after the First World War. It was a 30 x 100 km strip of land that allowed Poland access to the Baltic Sea.

Just before fleeing Feodor married Valentina Nikifrovna Berezovsky and later fathered Zinaida (Zena) who was born on November 10, 1921 in Danzig.

Feodor was born in 1892 in Vladikavkas in the Terskaya region of Georgia. He came from a well-to-do family that had land and a good income and were supporters of the Czarist government.

Czarist Officer

He chose a career in the Cavalry of the Russian army, distinguished himself and rose in the ranks and eventually became a Colonel and Divisional Commander prior to the Revolution. He was wounded five times in the First World War and won the Belgian Cross and the Order of St. George. During the Civil War after the Russian Revolution he was wounded nine times before escaping to Danzig. Feodor's parents and brother were killed by the communists and several other relatives disappeared.

Danzig harbour 1930s.

When Feodor arrived in Danzig he trained himself to be a mechanic and worked at that trade over the years. He was also involved with other so called White Russian soldiers (as compared to the Bolshevik Red Russians). They trained for future attempts to attack the communists in Russia.

After translating her father's and mother's diaries years later, Zena recalled the hardships of those times: "For eight solid months after I was born there were daily entries in my father's diary. Then he found work and that work was very physical doing construction. Later for weeks he was away as a mechanic on a small ship.

Life was very hard and cruel for my parents, leaving their country, their parents, relatives and friends, their language and

Feodor, Valentina and Zinaida Petschersky lived in exile from Russia in the Free City of Danzig in the Polish Corridor on the Baltic Sea in the 1930s.

The Polish Corridor and the Free City of Danzig provided access to the Baltic Sea to Poland between the two World Wars. The area was occupied by Germany during World War Two. After the defeat of Germany, many people fled to the West as the Russians advanced on Germany.

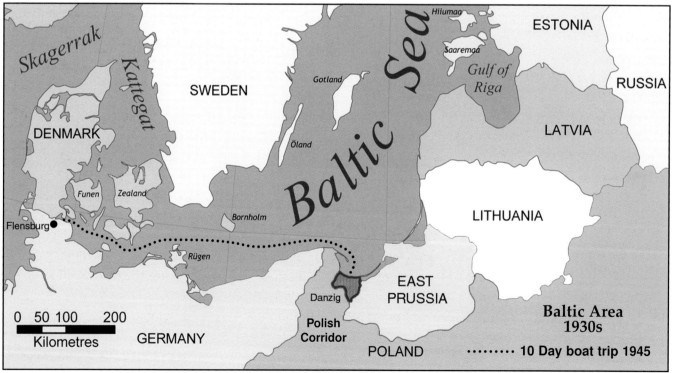

their way of life. My father's family had a fruit plantation in Russia, a good home and no worry about finances.

My father met my mother when she was eighteen. When they were married the revolutionary fighting was so close that my father's battalion was evacuated.

My mother never saw her parents again. A German soldier informed us that they had starved to death in 1933 during Stalin's regime."

A few letters were exchanged with Valentina; in one, her parents try to sound upbeat but ended with: "Actually, there is nothing good. Please write. We wait for news impatiently, let us hear from you, please."

Zena added: "It was very dangerous to write to Communist Russia because people with relatives in other countries were persecuted or sent to Siberia. This happened to my mother's brother. He was sent to do hard labour in Siberia. He was never involved in politics. His only crime was having a sister in a foreign country.

For a while we lived in a little cottage in a small village. My brother was born there. He had a weak heart and died at six weeks. I remember my parents walking along a train tracks with my father's arm over my mother's shoulder and crying."

Second World War

In 1939 Poland was occupied by the Nazis. Feodor, Valentina and Zena went through some terrible times. The Second World

Louise de Kirilene Lawrence
1894-1992

Louise de Kirilene Lawrence the famous author and Dionne Quint Nurse was a victim of the Russian Revolution like many others. She lived and wrote her many books in her log cabin on Pimisi Bay, in Calvin Township on the Mattawa River.

Louise came from a well-to-do Russian family. At the age of 17 she had a passion to experience life and trained to be a nurse. As a nurse she worked in Denmark at a camp for Russian Officers wounded by the Bolsheviks. She met Lieutenant Gleb de Kirilene, the son of a Russian general. They fell in love and were married. He returned to Russia to fight and was imprisoned. Louise followed him from camp to camp until he disappeared like many others into Siberia where he was never heard of again.

Louise came to Canada and became a Red Cross nurse in Bonfield. When the Dionne Quints were born in 1936 she became a lead nurse. She wrote a book *The Quints' First Year* and won the King George V Jubilee medal for her work with the Quints. She moved to Pimisi Bay and became a naturalist and wrote 500 reviews, 17 scientific papers, and 5 books. One of

Louise de Kirilene Lawrence and first husband from the cover of her book. (NHB)

those books was *Another Winter, Another Spring: A Love Remembered* the story of her relationship and unhappy ending with her Russian husband. The book is still in print and is in most local libraries. For a profile of Louise see my May 10, 2002 Heritage Perspective column on my website.

War had no precedent in human history. Millions of people died. Among them were 22 million Russians, 2.5 million Poles, 7 million Germans, 6 million Jews and several hundred thousand English, American and Canadian soldiers. Millions were displaced. The people of Baltic republics were particularly hard hit.

In another small diary (Translated from German) Zena made a few telling comments

about her past. When Germany declared war on September 1, 1939 as an eighteen-year-old, she wrote: "Today, Friday, at 5 o'clock in the morning I heard cannons for the first time—when will the last be? A feeling of dread has overtaken me, my hands are shaking. Mother is crying.

England declared war

Continued on page 24.

Danzig harbour after the German occupation. Note the swastika banners hanging on the buildings. Below are the Petschersky family passports issued by the Nazi authorities in occupied Danzig.

WHERE RIVERS MEET

When Germany invaded Russia Zena's father (left) joined his White Russian compatriots as part of the "Russian Liberation Army" in one last attempt to rid his homeland of the Communists.

Zena and her mother Valentina in their Danzig apartment. As early German victories turned to defeat they waited anxiously for news about father and husband Feodor.

Continued from page 21.

against Germany at 11 a.m. on Sunday. There is a constant noise from cannons and airplanes."

Invasion of Russia

When Germany invaded Russia Zena's father joined in one last attempt to rid his homeland of of the Communists. She wrote: "On July 22nd, 1941, at three o'clock in the morning, the war against Russia began. Father left on July 17th, 1941. One victory followed on the heels of the other. We were waiting with anxious hearts. How would all this end? The winter of 1942 was very hard, although it was much milder than that of 1941, when temperatures were -40º C to -50º C on average in Russia. Many froze to death, lost arms and legs. In January of 1943, the fighting became even more intense. Stalingrad was under siege. Everyone lives in anxious expectation."

Life in the War Zone

Zena made a few brief references to life in the war zone.

On November 27th, 1943 she wrote: "We have been at war for three years and five months now. A lot has happened during that time. We have forgotten what peace feels like. We no longer

know how to laugh. Every thought, every conversation revolves around the war. Poland, the Netherlands, Belgium, France, Norway, Yugoslavia and Greece are occupied."

On another occasion Valentina pulled Zena's arm up in a Nazi salute as soldiers

passed so she would not be noticed or worse.

During the war Zena worked hard and gained remarkable insights on the condition of people. Entries in her diary show a deep empathy for abused people. She wrote: "Since 1941,

Russian civilian prisoners of war have been brought here from Russia. Beautiful, strong and healthy people, but dressed very poorly. I have started working at a job placement office as an interpreter and minder for those *Ostarbeiter* (Eastern workers) as they are called. I see much suffering and grief every single day. It is so difficult to help."

She then added, surprisingly, considering her czarist and anti-communist background: "They are regarded as lesser people, as Bolshevists. But how can a nation help it if its leaders are bad people, criminals etc. No nation wants war, especially not the Russians! Of course, people of the younger generation have communist views—how could they not, not knowing anything else. But it is so easy to change these people— all the Russian soul requires to be won over is to be treated decently. But no, these people are treated very badly. Where will this lead?"

Displaced Persons

When the war came to a close the Petscherskys were relocated to a displaced persons camp in West Germany at Flensburg, Schleswig-Holstein near the Danish border. At the displaced persons camp Zena wrote about their trip there.

"My father is dying of his war wounds and cancer. The immeasurable disappointment of finally not being able to free his country and go home broke his will to live. We escaped Danzig on a ten day boat voyage to the West with no food or water."

On November 10, 1945 Valentina, on Zena's 24th birthday, wrote the following note in her diary: "A big tragedy has befallen us. We have lost your dear so loved father on October 23, 1945, one day before our 26th wedding day. He was not only a father to you, but a friend and you could discuss and share everything with him. He loved you terribly and was ready to give his life for you. Your father was very ill and suffered terribly from cancer for eleven months. You gave him morphine by injection and he called you his Doctor."

Canada

It took four years to arrange to get out of the refugee camp in Flensburg. At one point they were part of a group organized to go to Uruguay, in South America, but the organizer absconded with the funds.

Eventually they got permits and a contract to come to Canada (see over). In October 1949 they arrived at Bremen-Tirpitz, a quarantine camp maintained by the Red Cross, and soon left on a ship to Canada.

They arrived in Canada on October 26th. In her diary Zena talked about her arrival in Canada and her early experiences. She commented that she

Zena's father came back from Russia a defeated man, wounded and with cancer. He made it to the displaced persons camp in West Germany but soon died. Valentina and Zena were now on their own to find a new life after the War.

was lucky she had learned English and French, although Canadian French was a problem.

She noted: "We were placed in different households as a part of our contract on coming to Canada. All male emigrants, regardless of their education, were placed as farmhands and the women as maids. Mother

was placed in a rich home but the lady was on a diet and my poor mother was as hungry as she was in Europe.

The lady where I was placed was an alcoholic with two unbelievably spoiled children. One night the husband tried to come to my bedroom. I then got a job in a (Birks) jewellery store and

I.R.O. (B.Z.) FORM 44

BRITISH ZONE OF GERMANY—INTERNATIONAL REFUGEE ORGANISATION

Certificate of Eligibility

1. IRO Serial Number 403008   2. Area Office 920 Sub-Office   3. Date Issued 31 May 49
                                       Detmold

4. Names   PETSCHERSKI   Sinaia   —
            Surname   Christian Name   Middle Name

5. Place of Birth Danzig   Danzig   Free State Danzig
                  Town   Province   Country

6. Date of Birth 10 Nov 1921

7. Present Address Herford, Bielefelder Str. 40

8. No. of accompanying family members under 16 years of age   Nil

9. Country of last habitual residence   Danzig   Date left Jan 45

10. Reason for leaving   fled

11. Date arrived in British Zone of Germany   Jan 5

12. Occupation   Dressmaker

13. Description:—
    Height 172 cm   Weight 60 kg   Eyes blue   Hair blond
    Languages spoken: Russian, German, English, Polish, French

14. Signature of Refugee   Sinaida Petscherski

Within the mandate of I.R.O.
Eligible for Legal and Political
protection including repatriation
and resettlement.

... Officer
Date ... IRO Area Office

... has been found to be within the mandate of IRO and eligible for the
following services:—

Legal and Political Protection only
Legal and Political Protection including Repatriation
Legal and Political Protection including Repatriation or Resettlement

Within the mandate of I.R.O.
(Strike out items not applicable)   Eligible for Legal and Political
                                     protection including repatriation
16.   and resettlement.
                                     Signature of Eligibility Officer

17. Period of Validity   J.E. Howey

18. Date left British Zone   31.5.49   Eligibility Officer
                                          Date   911 IRO Area Office
19. Reason   J. E. HOWEY

20. The IRO Office should be notified of all current changes in the status of the person or address.

21. The bearer is entitled to care and maintenance in a Transit Camp only if accepted and called forward for repatriation or resettlement at IRO expense.

THIS CERTIFICATE IS NOT A PASS OR IDENTITY CARD

PSS(HQ)R3077/10M/2-49

After four years in a displaced persons camp in West Germany, Zena and her mother Valentina got the life altering authorization to "resettle" in Canada. As a condition they had to work as domestic servants for two years.

Zena and her mother Valentina finally arrived in Canada in 1949.

Zena met Dr. Firmin Monestime at a Christmas party in 1950. He charmed her with his conversation and laughter.

my mother in an old folks home. Things were looking up."

Zena was an attractive woman and there is some evidence that she had suitors. On one occasion she received a long touching letter from a gentleman who had an interest in her from her time in Europe. The following are a few brief sentences from his letter: "I don't know how you will react to my letter. Perhaps you are already married. I would be very unhappy if that were the case. Even though there is a danger that you might find this funny, I have to tell you that I have not been able to forget you. You live vibrantly and vivid in my memory.

Sometimes it seems to me that you only left a few days ago. There are certain things that have such an impact on your life that they stay with you and you

can not obtain closure. I hope that you and your lovely momma have settled in to your new life and home. Or, do you sometimes pine for your old life in Europe?"

Christmas Party

In 1950 Zena recalled that her mother and her were "invited to a large Christmas party with many medical doctors from various parts of the world."

One man, Dr. Firmin Monestime, intrigued her with his conversation and laughter. When they went to a club she found out he was an excellent dancer. He later invited her to a ball with some of his medical friends where he recited poetry, and charmed her. She wrote that on New Year's Eve she "had to make a wish—mine was—if this Black doctor asks me to marry

him—I will!"

Dr. Monestime was also interested in Zena but had to establish his practice first. In 1951, as mentioned earlier, he heard about the possibility of setting up practice in the isolated Northern Ontario town of Timmins and headed there with a colleague to have a look.

Firmin & Zena Monestime

4
The Doctor is In

"My practice was booming in no time and from then until now I've had no serious problems." Dr. Monestime, 1972

ON THAT FATEFUL DAY in the summer of 1951 when Dr. Monestime and his colleague Dr. G. Lamontagne stopped for a quick lunch at the Chez Francois restaurant in Mattawa Dr. Monestime did not have to worry about the owners not wanting him in their restaurant. Francois Martin, the owner, had been operated on by Dr. Monestime a few months earlier in Ottawa and remembered him.

"The celebrations started and the party shifted upstairs to the apartment over the restaurant, where I ended up sleeping," Dr. Monestime recalled.

A long standing Mattawa doctor had recently died and a replacement was badly needed. "They tried to tell me that I should open up a practice in Mattawa. I tried to tell them that I didn't have any resources." But the Martins and others persisted.

Dr. Monestime's fiancée Zena Petschersky lived in Ottawa and Mattawa was a lot closer than Timmins. He loved the beautiful setting of Mattawa, so he responded to the town's need. Francois Martin had an empty apartment above the store and a small space for a doctor's office. Dr. Monestime agreed to stay for a few weeks until the doctor shortage was resolved. His colleague headed for Timmins.

The Chez Francois Restaurant on Main Street in Mattawa. A vacant apartment was available upstairs and a room for an office was available in the basement.

The next day the local car dealer Fred Lafreniere visited Dr. Monestime and said there was a car (a Cadillac) for him in the driveway. Dr. Monestime said he had no money but Fred said he could pay when he could. This generosity and other welcoming behaviour encouraged the doctor and he soon opened an office in the basement of the restaurant and was busy with patients in his office and at the hospital. It also turned out that the Roman Catholic Sisters who ran the Mattawa General Hospital knew him from Ottawa.

He made regular trips to Ottawa to visit his fiancée Zena Petschersky and their relationship flourished.

Marriage

Firmin and Zena married in Zena's Russian Orthodox Church in Ottawa. Firmin was 43 and

Dr. Monestime in his office in 1953. He was soon busy with patients in his office and at the Mattawa General Hospital where he was regularly on-call. It turned out the Sisters of Charity who ran the hospital knew him from Ottawa.

Valentina (centre) with Firmin and Zena on their wedding day.

Firmin and Zena were married in Zena's Russian Orthodox Church in Ottawa.

WHERE RIVERS MEET

Daughter Valentina (Vala) was born in 1953.

Firmin (centre) visited and corresponded regularly with Haitian friends in Canada including Dr. Hypolyte (right) and Dr. Wiss who practiced in Sudbury.

Zena was 32. She moved to Mattawa and they decided to stay and raise a family. A daughter Valentina (Vala) was born in 1953 and a son Feodor (Fedia) in 1954.

Zena's mother Valentina was welcomed into the household. The children called her "Babie" which is a short form of *Baboushka*, Russian for grandmother. The town was a bit slow adjusting to the handsome Black doctor with the beautiful blond wife, but the hardworking capa-bilities and personalities of the family soon won over the town.

Medical Practice

Dr. Monestime was not long in Mattawa before his practice grew both in his office and at the hospital where he was regularly on-call. He served people beyond Mattawa and had a reputation for visiting people at home for their convenience when ill.

His reputation for availability and caring spread. He had a remarkable relationship with many families and often visited late into the night when on-call at the hospital.

When asked by a reporter in 1972 whether race had ever been a problem he replied: "My practice was booming in no time and from then until now I've had no serious problems. You might find a very few—and not the most intelligent—who may say they won't come to see me because of my race. But very few."

Sometimes children would

In early 1954 Dr. Monestime opened a new clinic in the former CWL Hall on Highway 17. Dr. Monestime is seen with Rhea Guilbeault R.N. in one of the clinics rooms (left). Nurse Guilbeault answers a phone call in the reception room while a patient waits for her appointment with the doctor (right).

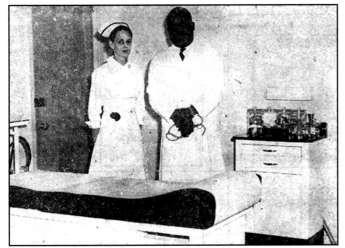

look temporarily disconcerted when meeting him for the first time, thinking his hands were dirty. He would laugh and rub his skin to show the child that they were not dirty.

Dr. Monestime was always improving his skills. He had completed some graduate work from England in 1948 and he did some more from the Royal Victoria College in Montreal in 1954. In 1956 he did a year of graduate study in Scotland while Zena and her mother Valentina remained in Mattawa with the two children.

Caring Doctor

Many people interviewed for this book told personal stories of Dr. Monestime's skills and character as a doctor.

One man had been at the scene of a fatal car-bus accident on the Trans-Canada Highway near Mattawa. A passer-by took the man and a seriously injured woman to a nearby first aid station. In short order Dr. Monestime arrived, checked them and drove them to the Mattawa Hospital where he supervised their medical requirements.

The man met Dr. Monestime in the late 1960s at a political convention and thanked him for his care and compassion. Dr. Monestime had no memory of the event but the man has a paragraph in his memoirs telling of the generous assistance he received.

Another man had polio as a child and had trouble walking. He was told he would be con-

In 1956 Firmin went to Scotland to study leaving Zena and Valentina with daughter Vala and new son Feodor (Fedia).

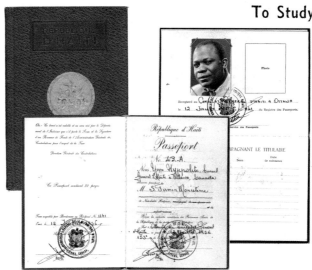

To Study in England

Dr. Firmin Monestime of Mattawa will leave August 27 for England where he intends to take advanced studies.

Dr. Monestime has had a general practice in Mattawa since 1951.

He will sail aboard the Scythia from Quebec City. Even before he leaves, Dr. Monestime is looking forward to his return to Mattawa.

Dr. Monestime's wife and children, Valentine, 3, and Theodore, 2, will stay in Mattawa while he is abroad.

Dr. Monestime expects to be in Europe for approximately one year.

Dr. Monestime was not yet a Canadian Citizen when he went to Scotland. He had to update his Haitian Passport in order to travel.

fined to a wheelchair and was told to visit Dr. Monestime. When he did the doctor got on the phone to The Hospital for Sick Children in Toronto and fought, at great length, the resistance to the child's acceptance there. Dr. Monestime finally turned to the young patient and told him to report to Toronto the next week. It changed the child's life and he led a normal life with

a family and steady employment thereafter and he never forgot Dr. Monestime's efforts on his behalf.

Beside the hundreds of routine visits in his office and in the hospital there were many other occasions where he would have to travel to isolated locations to provide help or certify death.

On one occasion, for example, Dr. Monestime took a call

WHERE RIVERS MEET

STUDYING IN SCOTLAND

Photos from Firmin's trip to Scotland show him wandering alone and studying hard. On the back of the photo at left he expresses pride in eating a meal that he cooked himself.

This postcard shows a spectacular view of Edinburgh Castle.

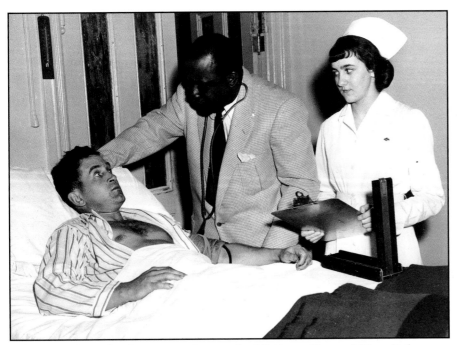

Dr. Monestime checks on a patient at the Mattawa General Hospital.

that a man on an island on the Ottawa River 37 kilometres north of Mattawa had collapsed. Lionel Tremblay recalls driving Dr. Monestime to as close as possible on the Ontario side where Dr. Monestime got a boat ride across to the victim.

Lionel drove the car home. A plane arrived with a nurse and Dr. Monestime and the nurse took the patient to North Bay where he was cared for. The Monestime family remembers a plane landing at their cottage returning Dr. Monestime to Mattawa. Apparently the patient and Dr. Monestime became friends and met on occasion.

There is evidence that the

After being away in Scotland, Dr. Monestime was happy to be back with his family in Canada. Here he is with Vala, Fedia and mother-in-law Valentina enjoying an afternoon at the cottage.

Doctor often did not get paid, or got paid over a period of time or was paid with food from a garden or a hunt.

Family Life

Sons Yura and Sasha were born in 1961 and 1962 and the children were soon a part of the active community with their interests in sports and music.

Dr. Monestime accepted the Russian influence in his family's life, and attended the Russian Orthodox Church and celebrated Russian customs with his family. Russian was spoken in the family home, along with French and English. Dr. Monestime, however, did not learn to speak Russian. The children were trilingual and baptized Russian Orthodox. Once grown up and married, Zena and Firmin's children followed custom and named their children with Russian names. They celebrated their Russian heritage in other ways.

Zena and her mother Valentina were like sisters and were inseparable. While both were very sensitive and caring women they had a toughness when necessary based on their previous survival experience during the turmoil of revolution and war before they came to Canada.

Valentina lived with the family in her own quarters and played her complicated role with finesse. Valentina and Zena did not work outside the home so both helped with the household chores and the raising of the children. In the 1960s and 70s Zena did the bookkeeping for Firmin.

In 1961 son Yura was born. Seen here are Vala (left), Fedia (right) and Yura.

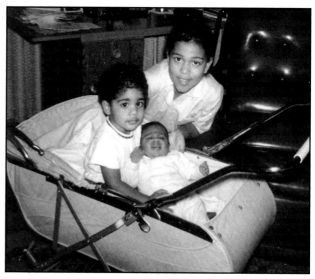

In 1962 son Sasha was born. Seen here are Vala (right), Yura (left) and Sasha.

The potential for problems did not materialize and they played their roles remarkably well. Both were dearly loved by the children.

With their support, Firmin who was a loving and caring father, was freed up to some extent to pursue his extensive medical practice, his soon to be active political life and his need to be involved in the community. There were undoubtedly some difficult times, as is the case in most families, but generally to the credit of all concerned, their family life worked well.

The children would on occasion visit Valentina's apartment and have her ear for advice, consolation and encouragement. Valentina had a few good friends and loved her garden and her family. Evidence from all quarters indicates that Dr. Monestime loved and honoured Valentina.

Joie de Vivre

It should be mentioned that Dr. Monestime is also remembered for his *joie de vivre* as well

as his serious approach to medicine, politics and family. He loved to get together with the boys at the Mattawa House and elsewhere for a few drinks, conversation, and some cards.

The story is often told of Dr. Monestime getting up from the table to help an inebriated

Dr. Monestime's first car in Mattawa was a Cadillac and after that he developed a penchant for them. (Below) One time he lost his car in a bet at the Mattawa House Hotel, one of his regular rendezvous (right).

patron get to the bathroom and back. When he returned to his friends at the table they were speechless. Dr. Monestime said: "Every man deserves respect no matter what his position or condition in life is."

On another occasion, after a long card game, Dr. Monestime had a good hand and no cash so he put up his Cadillac to cover the bet—and walked home.

Another often repeated quirk was Dr. Monestime's regular use of other peoples' cigarettes, often walking away with the pack. I only heard one story where it backfired. A woman found her cigarettes gone and went into a meeting to get them back. When Dr. Monestime chastised her she chastised him equally and was not bothered again. They remained friends.

Citizenship

In the mid 1950s Zena and Valentina received their Canadian citizenship. In 1958 Firmin received his Canadian citizenship. At his citizenship ceremony the judge asked Dr. Monestime to give some remarks he said: "I am ready to give my life for this country if I have to. I also expect to enjoy all the rights of this country and I do not want to be considered as a second-class citizen." Soon he would embark on a career in politics that would make Canadian history.

Zena Monestime's Canadian citizenship documents from 1955 (Top). Firmin did not get his citizenship until 1958 where he was asked to speak on behalf of the new citizens. (Below, he is at centre right wearing fedora.)

New Canadian Citizens Welcomed

New Canadian citizens gather on the steps of the court house following Tuesday's citizenship ceremony. Judge J. A. S. Plouffe (in the foreground) presided. Mayor Merle Dickerson, Red Cross officials and representatives of the four IODE chapters attended the service and extended a welcome to the new citizens. —Nugget Staff Photo

The soft buzz of conversation was in half a dozen languages preceeding a special sitting of the district court Tuesday when 31 new Canadians received their very many liberties," Judge Plouffe told the group.

"We have no Gestapo and brainwashing is unknown to us," he continued. The judge

Dr. S. F. Monestime of Mattawa, spoke on behalf of the new Canadians. He said those taking their citizenship would be in the "front seat" in war or in peace."

WHERE RIVERS MEET

Photo Album One:
Family Life

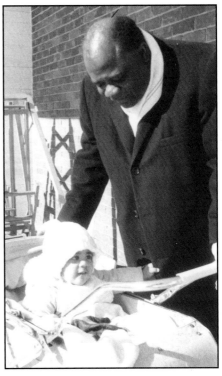

With Yura

Firmin with the children

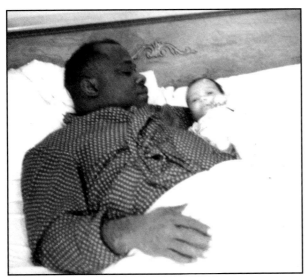

With Vala

With Vala, Fedia, Yura, Sasha and Zena

With Vala

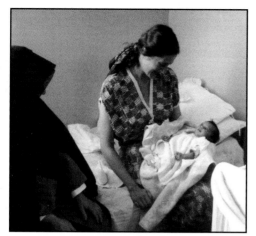

Zena and Vala

Babie and Vala

Fedia and Vala

Fedia and Vala

Yura and Sasha

Vala

Sasha and Yura at Russian Easter table

Sasha, Yura, Fedia and Vala

Relaxing at the Cottage

Monestime house in the 1970s

Babie was known for her flowers

People of . .
MATTAWA

Vote For The Man Who Put Mattawa On The Map

RE-ELECT

Dr. F. Monestime
MAYOR

RE-ELISEZ

Dr. F. Monestime
MAIRE

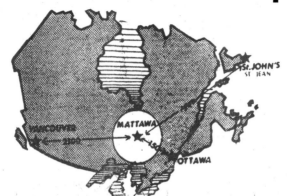

In the past you have voted for me. I have used all my connections, and my energy to give you low-cost housing, better street lighting, paving and road maintenance. In one word, I have done my best to put Mattawa on the way of modern progress.

If you are in favor of real progress, I ask that you once again give me your support.

Better recreation facilities are needed for our young people. Those people who are raising families should be able to count on stable taxes. For those people who are retired, there should be low-cost housing and other facilities available.

There should be better parks for our citizens and for our visitors. We want those visitors to return to us.

My work on the national scene has helped me to put Mattawa on the map. The contacts I have made have been invaluable. I know people from the Yukon to Labrador and now they know where Mattawa is.

In the search for industry, and in the work of receiving government assistance, it is not enough just to write letters. You must know where to go, who to see, what door to knock upon.

To have ample time on one's hands is not the only qualification needed to be Mattawa's mayor. Your mayor needs honesty, integrity, devotion, experience and knowledge. He must represent and work for everyone in the community.

As a medical doctor, I can assure you that while acting as mayor of Mattawa, I have never missed a call from a patient. My professional work and my civic functions do not conflict. In fact, I find participating in municipal affairs offers relaxation.

I thank the voters of Mattawa for supporting me in the past. I have tried my best to serve you well. On Monday, I ask that you once again do your duty and cast your vote. Your support will enable me to carry on the job, to use my knowledge, my experience and to call upon my many friends across Canada for the betterment of Mattawa.

Vote for Monestime. He stands for the future.

Dans le passé, vous m'avez élu. Je me suis servi de toutes mes connaissances et toute mon énergie pour vous obtenir des habitations à prix modiques, un meilleur éclairage de rues, l'asphaltage et un meilleur maintien des chemins.

Si vous desirez vraiment le progrès, je vous demande encore une fois de me donner votre appui.

Nous avons besoin de meilleurs facilités recreatives pour nos jeunes. Ceux qui élèvent leur famille doivent pouvoir compter sur un niveau de taxes qui demeurera stable. Pour ceux qui sont à leur retraite, nous devrions avoir des logements à prix modiques et d'autres facilités disponibles.

Nous devrons avoir de meilleurs parcs à la disposition de nos citoyens et de nos visiteurs. Nous voulons que ces visiteurs nous reviennent.

Mon travail sur le plan national a fait connaitre Mattawa. Les contacts que j'ai faits sont de grande valeur. J'ai rencontré des gens de tous les coins du pays, du Yukon au Labrador et ceux-ci savent maintenant où se situe la ville de Mattawa.

Dans la recherche pour de l'industrie et dans le travail en faveur de recevoir des octrois du gouvernement, il n'est pas suffisant d'écrire des lettres. Il faut savoir comment se présente.

Avoir du temps n'est pas le seul qualificatif necessaire a la mairie de Mattawa. Votre maire doit posséder l'hônneteté, l'integrité, l'expérience et les connaissances necessaires.

Comme medécin, je vous assure que je n'ai jamais manqué un appel auprès d'un patient. Au contraire, j'ai trouvé que les affaires municipales étaient pour moi du repos.

Je remercie les électeurs de Mattawa pour m'avoir élu dans le passé. J'ai fait de mon mieux pour être votre serviteur fidèle. Je vous demande encore une fois de faire votre devoir de citoyens lundi prochain et d'aller voter.

Votez pour Monestime. Son programme aidera l'avenir de Mattawa.

On Monday, December 2nd VOTE . . .
Monestime
MAYOR

X

5
Political Career

"As for the Black man, the gynecologist who treats the women and the mayor who runs the town's affairs, there just doesn't seem to be any problem. It almost makes you wonder why you asked."- Toronto Sun 1972

WITH HIS CONCERN for people and his belief in change it was not long before Dr. Monestime became interested in local politics. In spite of being quite liberal in his views he gravitated toward the Progressive Conservative Party after meeting Ontario Premier Leslie Frost in the mid 1950s. Frost was in Mattawa campaigning for Conservative candidate and MPP John Chaput. Prime Minister John Diefenbaker's support for the Canadian Bill of Rights which was passed in 1960 also influenced his decision to support the PC's. Dr. Monestime became active in the Mattawa Progressive Conservative Association and Zena became involved in the Women's group.

With his medical practice established and his family maturing he made a careful move to run for Mattawa Council. In those days the term was for one year. He won a council seat in 1962.

First Black Mayor

Having gained confidence, experience, and credibility, he ran in the fall of 1963 to be the Mayor in 1964. On

Dr. Monestime stands at the head of Mattawa's Main Street. On the left is the former location of the Chez Francois Restaurant.

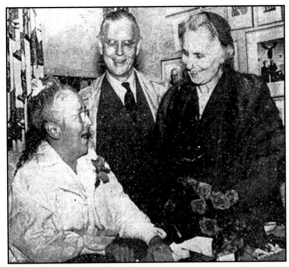

Ontario Premier Leslie Frost and his wife visit with pioneer Mattawa resident Mrs. K. McKechnie, owner of the Mattawa House Hotel, while campaigning for John Chaput.

Zena Monestime (top right) joined the Mattawa Women's Progressive Conservative Association. Seen here are: (front row L to R) Mrs. Morel, treasurer; Hilda Millen, president; Marcelle Lafreniere, secretary; (back row L to R) Mrs. Ross, vice-president; Mrs. Davidson, Doreen Floyd and Zena, conveners.

Tuesday, November 12, 1963 he won the election making history as the first Black mayor elected in Canada and probably in North America. The *North Bay Nugget* commented that: "Mayor-elect Dr. Firmin Monestime, a very active political figure, brings vigour and enterprise to council deliberations." He won the election again 1964. On both occasions he beat longstanding and well respected Salem Turcotte. Mr. Turcotte became a friend and supporter of Dr. Monestime.

Dr. Monestime was elected mayor at the same time as the United States was experiencing a violent struggle against racism and for civil rights. Dr. Monestime's daughter Vala remembers when Dr. Martin Luther King Jr. made his "I have a dream" speech in August 1963. Her father was watching with the family when King referred to his four children and said that he dreamed that they would "one day live in a nation where they will not be judged by the color of their skin, but by the content of their character." Dr. Monestime

In December 1962 Dr. Monestime was elected for the first time as a councillor in the 1963 town council where he won the most votes. Here he is checking election returns with town hall secretary Pierrette Burke and other first time winner J. Arsidas Serre.

Like Dr. King, Dr. Monestime had "four little children" Yura, Vala, Fedia and Sasha in 1963.

turned to his four children and said that the same applied to them. He was elected mayor only three months later.

With the wide national and international recognition Dr. Monestime received as the first Black mayor in Canada, one wonders about the impact of his colour on his life in Canada.

In various newspaper articles Dr. Monestime talked about some of the racial incidents in his life. On one occasion he recalled hearing someone at a rally say that you should not shake his hand because it was dirty.

During the 1969 Mattawa Town Council election where Dr. Monestime was running for Mayor and which he won by a landslide there was a widely reported minor racial incident. A Mattawa man and his two sons wrote about 100 notes that said: "People of Mattawa beware. Do not vote Black." Some were written on blank order forms from the Liquor Store. The notes appeared in various locations the same night that Dr. Monestime appeared on the CBC program Take 30 with Adrienne Clarkson. Some thought he got extra votes because of the incident.

The OPP criticized the national press for publicizing the incident saying it was minor and that no names were mentioned. The men were found but not identified. Dr. Monestime said "I haven't seen anything like that in 19 years." There are undoubtedly incidents that remain untold, but with his forward-looking and confident approach to life he simply moved on, as many peo-

Dr. Monestime reacts to favourable poll results.

ple do, if confronted with issues of gender, age and nationality.

To paraphrase the "I have a dream" speech, Mattawa did not judge Dr. Monestime by the colour of his skin but by the content of his character.

In interviews with people in Mattawa there were various

Dr. Monestime received this photograph and congratulations from the Haitian Embassy. The note reads. "To my excellent friend and compatriot, Dr. S. F. Monestime, who has honoured our country (Haiti) in Canada. Cordially, Philippe Cantave."

opinions about why he was so popular.

Certainly the fact that he was a highly capable general practitioner, surgeon and gynecologist was an overriding factor. His confident and direct approach showed no vulnerability that allowed for intolerance. He was remarkably well dressed, drove a Cadillac, and had an infectious and welcoming laugh.

He also had an ever present sense of justice and fairness. He treated all people equally and loved to spend time with them and to work for them. His strong and contributing family was another significant factor.

Several sources commented that one of the main reasons Dr. Monestime was accepted was that the people of Mattawa were so open. They certainly deserve a lot of credit and are an important part of the equation unlike in some other areas of the world where even if white people accept Blacks they are often considered second class citizens.

Continued on page 46.

Canadian life better than any

EDITOR'S NOTE: This story about Dr. Monestime was written by THE NUGGET at the request of The Canadian Press. The news agency distributed the story to all papers in Ontario for release on Feb. 5 (today). One Northern Ontario paper, however, violated the release date and published the story on Tuesday of this week.

By JEAN GUY BIGRAS
Nugget District Editor

MATTAWA — Discrimination, virtually unknown in Northern Ontario, would be practised if more colored people infiltrated the area. This is the opinion of Dr. S. F. Monestime, mayor of this community of 3,500 people, the only colored person to hold such a high municipal office in Canada.

Dr. Monestime, who was born in Haiti and came to Canada in 1941, states that discrimination originates with American influence in Canada and parents' fear that their daughters will marry Negroes. He said that segregation is practised in Canadian areas where the Negro population is high, such as in the Owen Sound district of Ontario and in New Brunswick.

Moreover, discrimination is very common among Ontario tourist operators, states Dr. Monestime. "This is caused by the American influence," explains the doctor. "Hotel and resort owners are afraid to lose American business if they allow Negroes in their establishments. They hang the "no

Dr. S. F. Monestime is a Haitian-born Negro who is serving his second term as mayor of Mattawa, On He is married to Zina Petschersky, a native of Poland and a direct descendant of Czarist Russians. Th met when he was a resident doctor at the Ottawa General Hospital. With them are their four children: ba row, Vala, 11(left) and Fedia, 10; front row, Sasha, 2, on his mother's lap, and Yura, 4.

—Nugget Staff Pho

ognized Dr. Monestime as the er enters his own mind wh n cize

The visiting black doctor who stayed to become mayor

MATTAWA, Ont. (UPI) — When you ask Dr. S. F. Monestime whether his electoral successes have been based on winning the black vote, he lets loose a deep, hearty laugh.

There is nothing strikingly unusual about Monestime, really, other than the fact that is both black and the mayor of the town of Mattawa.

While he doesn't find the community unusual, an outsider might.

Mattawa, snuggled comfortably in the hills between the Ottawa and Mattawa rivers, about 200 miles northwest of Ottawa, is home to 3,000 persons, 2,997 of them white.

Monestime, a high school teacher and another doctor make up the town's black population.

The doctor left Haiti, his native country, in the 1940s. After studying medicine in various parts of Scotland, the United States and Canada, he settled in Mattawa in 1951.

He ran for town council in 1963, winning easily. Since then he has run for councillor once and mayor four times, winning handily each time, sometimes with a majority of three to one.

He is not just a country bumpkin — on a wider political scale he has also been a national director of the Progressive Conservative Party.

"I didn't intend to come here," he said, looking out his office window and down the main street.

"I was coming up to another Northern town to visit a doctor friend who had opened an office there. I stopped in Mattawa to eat —

But it turned out that the manager, (a man named Armand Tremblay who has since moved to Ottawa) had been operated on by Monestime some months earlier in an Ottawa hospital and remembered him.

"The celebrations started and the party shifted upstairs to the apartment over the restaurant, where I ended up sleeping," Monestime said.

"They tried to tell me that I should open up a practice in Mattawa, but I tried to tell them that I didn't have any resources. I didn't even own a car."

His protests went unheeded. His new friends took him to the local car dealership where they backed his loan to buy a car, and soon after he opened his office in the basement of the restaurant before shifting to more suitable quarters.

Race relations? "My practice was booming in no time and from then until now I've had no serious problems.

"You might find a very few — and not the most intelligent — who may say they won't come to see me because of my race. But very few."

And if 20 cars go by Monestime's office while he is bidding the visitor goodbye, the occupants of 19 of them lean out their windows in passing and yell their greetings to the mayor.

More than half of them are French-Canadian, and the others English-Canadian, two groups who don't always live in total harmony in

Dr. Monestime, Mattawa's mayor: "I've had no serious problems."

Negro Mayor Fulfills Of Canadian Allegic

MATTAWA, Ont. (CP)—When Dr. S. F. Monestime, a Haitian-born Negro, took the oath of allegiance as a Canadian citizen in 1958, he said:

"I am ready to give my life for this country if I have to. I also expect to enjoy all rights of this country and I do not want to be considered as a second-class citizen."

His expectation appears to have been fulfilled in this town 35 miles east of North Bay. A first-class citizen, he now is serving his second term as mayor.

A general practitioner and surgeon, Dr. Monestime came to Canada from his native Haiti in 1941 and began practising medicine here 10 years later.

He became interested in municipal politics, was elected top councillor in 1963 and mayor in 1964. He was re-elected by an overwhelming majority for this year.

An ardent Progressive Conservative, the 55-year-old doc-

ican influence. Hotel and resc owners are afraid to lose Ame ican business if they allow N groes in their establishment They hang the 'no vacanc sign as soon as colored peop try to get accommodation."

A chance meeting led D Monestime to set up practice this community of 3,500. Wi Dr. Gaston Lamontagne, he wa heading for Timmins, Ont where both doctors were open an office. They stopped e route at a Mattawa restaurar Fred Tremblay, owner of th business, recognized Dr. Mone time as the man who had pe formed surgery on him in C tawa a few years earlier.

Mr. Tremblay convinced D Monestime of the need for second medical practitioner i Mattawa. Dr. Lamontagne cor tinued to Timmins alone.

"Mattawa has been good 1 me and I intend to work for th interests of the community, says Dr. Monestime.

As mayor, he already ha

ays Mattawa MD

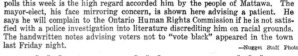

onestime applied to be-
medical officer in the
States Army, but never
a reply. He was award-
n-American Scholarship
in New York, but did

he completed a year of post-
graduate studies at Edinburgh,
Scotland.

EDUCATION

According to the former resi-

become more active in federal
politics.

"If I were called to the position, I would be proud to become Prime Minister of Ca-
ada. This is the country I love."

egro immigrant town's top citizen

WA (CP) — When
. Monestime, a Hai-
Negro, took the oath
ance as a Canadian
1958, he said:
ready to give my
is country if I have
expect to enjoy all
this country and I

come Prime Minister of Canada," he says. "This is the
country I love. I want to serve
it well."

He finds racial discrimination virtually unknown in northern Ontario but feels it
would develop if more colored
people moved into the area.

"Mattawa has been good to
me, and I intend to work for
the interests of the community," says Dr. Monestime

Mr. Tremblay convinced Dr.
Monestime of the need for a
second medical practitioner in
Mattawa. Dr. Lamontagne continued to Timmins alone.

cal officer on the international
route between Haiti and the
Dominican Republic. He was
on duty during the massacre
of 50,000 Haitians, ordered by
Dominican president Dr. Raphael Trujillo, 1937 and 1938.

"I saw all kinds of broken
bodies. I helped bury the dead

he says. "I was afraid for
my life."

He applied for permission to
study in Quebec City, which
was granted. In 1941, he left
his country quietly, without
announcing his departure, for
fear of reprisals.

ducation, housing highlights
f Mattawa mayor's '65 address

TTAWA (Staff) — Educa-
ousing and planning high-
the program for 1965
d by Mayor Dr. S. F.
stime in his inaugural ad-
on Monday.

mayor commented on the
nistration which sparked
ss in 1964, adding that for
rst time in many years,
to a 100 per cent tax col-
n was recorded. He added
the municipality did not
w a single penny from the
to administer its affairs
4.

plaining his program for
coming year, Dr. Mones-
pointed out that, despite a
al by the electorate in the
14 elections for the con-
ion of a museum-library,
till hopes to establish a
cipal library. "We must
forward for our youth, for
ation, and I think that a
ry is foremost in educa-
" said the mayor.

other projects, the mayor
mentioned plans for im-
ements to the existing park,
street lights and neces-
repairs to streets and
tings.
e are all united for a com-
good cause, whether rich
oor, sick or in health. We
ook at man as a human

being, with a spirit, a heart
and a formation: this is the
principle of democracy," said
the mayor.

The mayor went on to say
that the community must have
men who get together and work
for the common good. These
leaders must understand the
need of others, as a group.

SOCIA

council meetings. They said they
will be asking many questions
and Mr. St. Eloi asked the other
members to please co-operate
and elp him gather as much
knowdge as possible.
Councillors Ejner Pedersen

and Vianney Sauve said they
will continue the work already
started by council and asked
fellow members to support their
efforts. They also sought the
co-operation of the general public.

One of the reasons for Dr. Firmin Monestime's overwhelming success at the
polls this week is the high regard accorded him by the people of Mattawa. The
mayor-elect, his face mirroring concern, is shown here advising a patient. He
says he will complain to the Ontario Human Rights Commission if he is not satis-
fied with a police investigation into literature discrediting him on racial grounds.
The handwritten notes advising voters not to "vote black" appeared in the town
last Friday night.
—Nugget Staff Photo

* * *   * * *   * * *

3 admit anti-black notes

(Continued from Page One)

Personality

Black mayor elected despite note blitz

Special to The Star

MATTAWA — This north-
ern Ontario town of 3,000

The Haitian who came to lunch and stayed to be mayor

By Richard Pierre

aning

Oath

as named medical
the international
Haiti and the Do-
ublic. He was on
the massacre of
ns, ordered by Do-
sident Dr. Raphael
937 and 1938.
kinds of broken
ped bury the dead
s pull bodies from

truce, in 1938, Dr.
eceived the Haitian
rit and Honor from
ie Lescot. He was
e medical position
ince.

began public criti-
he termed deplor-
s in his homeland,
uential families in
Eventually he re-
te medical officer.
F MONEY
you become an
e state as soon as
e civil service," he
afraid for my life."
for permission to

At first it wasn't easy talking to St. Fermin Monestime. The 50-yard walk down
Main Street from the Mattawa Hotel to
where his 1970 green Caddy was parked
was a journey that took time. House-
wives, little kids, a lumber salesman, no
one passed by without stopping for a
piece of conversation. "Coming to the
game tonight, Doc?" . . . "You will present the trophy, won't you, Doc?" . . .
"About that meeting, Doc . . ."

St. Fermin Monestime was in no rush.

"They weren't that sympathetic when
I first came," says Monestime later. He
chuckles. The Caddy's air conditioning
purrs. The thick timberland of the upper
Ottawa valley flashes by. "Today they
love me."

One of Mattawa's four physicians,
Monestime is both open and reticent at
once. His arrival 21 years ago in the
small Ontario lumber town, 40 miles
from North Bay on the Ontario-Quebec
border, is a local legend. He was driving
through, stopped for lunch, and never
left.

The mayor of Mattawa (pop. 3,000) for
more than four years, all told, Monestime is one of Ontario's two national directors of the Progressive Conservative
Party of Canada. He is also black. The
only negro mayor in Canada, when he
was first elected in 1964.

Born the son of a wealthy tanner 59
years ago on the Caribbean island of
Haiti, Monestime was a fellow medical
student of the late Papa Doc Duvalier.

"People ask why I came here," says Mayor Monestime of Mattawa. "Just look at this scenery. It's like being on holiday all the time."

In the summer of '38 just after he had
graduated from the Port au Prince fac-
ulty of medicine, Monestime went to
work as a government doctor on the border of Haiti and the Dominican Republic. Shortly after he found himself in the
middle of a bloody war between the two
countries, which claimed the lives of
10,000 Haitians. For his work with the
wounded he was decorated as an officer
of the Order of Honor and Merit.

In 1944 Monestime resigned from government service. He wanted to go to

woman who'd only been in Canada for
three months — "but who spoke better
English than me," says Monestime.

In 1951 St. Firmin headed out for
Timmins in a battered old jalopy and
with $10 in his pocket. His plans for set-
ting up practice there, however, never
materialized. Stopping for lunch in Mattawa, he discovered that the restaurant
owner was an old patient of his from Ottawa. "He persuaded me that Mattawa
was the place to live," says Monestime.
"I stayed."

tended garden out front. He pointed
again. "See, just down from the liquor
store." A chuckle. "I'm a man of rum
and Coke."

When Monestime first set up practice
in Mattawa 21 years ago he had no problems building a practice. "On the street
people would stare at me," says Monestime. "They were curious. But when
people are sick and need a doctor they
don't stop to consider if he's black."

Monestime became interested in politics in 1955 after meeting Leslie Frost, a

Continued from page 43.

Mattawa has been widely recognized for its full acceptance of Dr. Monestime and his family to the present day.

In an article in the *Toronto Sun* in 1972, one of numerous articles on him being the first Black, or "negro," mayor, the writer asked about race relations and then stated in his last paragraph: "But as for the Black man, the gynecologist who treats the women and the mayor who runs the town's affairs, there just doesn't seem to be any problem. It almost makes you wonder why you asked."

For more on Black history see Appendix 2 and see article by *Toronto Star* columnist Gary Lautens on page 48.

After a two year hiatus for a battle with prostate cancer which he won, Dr. Monestime returned to politics and came back as a councillor in 1968 and 69. He was mayor again in 1970, 71, 72, 73 and 74 and in the two year terms 1975-76 and 1977-78. With three years as councillor and nine times as mayor he was active for 14 years.

Progressive Politics

Over the years Dr. Monestime led Council through much progress. On one occasion he described his philosophy as "improve, improve, improve." All change involved the cooperation of Council and the changes were a credit to everyone. He championed the building of low rental housing and the improvement of existing housing. He encouraged indus-

The Monestime family around the time of Dr. Monestime's election as mayor. Left to right are: Zena, Yura, Sasha, Firmin, Vala and Fedia.

try and road and street improvements as well as dealing with numerous day to day issues.

On one occasion Dr. Monestime took a strong stand on the replacement for a vacant council seat strongly supporting the runner-up candidate in the previous election which is the usual practice. Other councillors wanted to bring someone else from the community. Dr. Monestime perceived intolerable bias and walked out and said he would resign.

He always represented Mattawa well at graduations, openings and meetings. The photo shows him at the raising of the new Canadian flag in 1965 when it was approved. He had a real enjoyment in these events and often dressed up for them as shown in this book.

People remember a Donkey Baseball event where players rode donkeys and left everyone laughing. Dr. Monestime rode donkeys in his front line work in Haiti's struggle against the Dominican Republic. He was one of the first on a donkey at the baseball game and he and everyone else enjoyed it immensely.

Dr. Monestime especially enjoyed visits from other politicians especially if they were of the Progressive Conservative persuasion. Prime Minister John Diefenbaker met him as did Ontario Premieres John Robarts

Mayor Monestime talks to Lorne Maeck the MPP for Parry Sound in front of some of Mattawa's new low rental housing units.

Mayor Monestime raising the new Canadian Flag at the Mattawa Town Hall in 1965. In the background are students in front of the Mattawa Public School.

The 1974 Mattawa Town Council: (L to R) Councillors Salem Turcotte and Joffre Jodouin, Mayor S. F. Monestime, Councillor and Deputy Mayor Mel Edwards, Councillors Annie Lamont and Fred Bangs and Clerk-Treasurer Louis Villeneuve. Missing is Councillor Joe St. Eloi.

People make the difference in Mattawa
Gary Lautens-Toronto Star column 1964

Canadians are so preoccupied with their "differences" these days that they forget people like Dr. Firmin Monestime even exist.

Dr. Monestime is the Mayor of Mattawa, a town of 4,000 located about 200 miles from Ottawa. Originally the Algonquin settled the village, "at the beautiful meeting place of the water," as they called it then.

And the Indian is still there. So are nearly 3,000 French Canadians and another 1,000 English Canadians. At least that is how the population is broken down today. People are tagged and put in packages.

But the doctor doesn't think that way.

He just calls them people. He figures they work and they worry and they play and they take care of their kids and they think about buying a new boat and they swear when their car gets stuck in the snow and they gossip and they go to church and they get indigestion and they try to do their best and . . .

Well, they are just like you and I.

Likes it Here

Dr. Monestime didn't win the election because he appealed to one bloc of voters or because he made sure he sat in the front row at Mass or because he spouted hate and division.

He is nobody's "man". Just his own - and everybody's.

He is not French Canadian. He is not English Canadian. In fact, he only came to this country in the late 40s to do post graduate work in medicine. He liked it and he stayed.

"Maybe I am a deeper Canadian than you," he said over the telephone.

He is not Catholic - but the Catholic population elects him. He is

Gary Lautens

a member of the Russian Orthodox Church, such a small segment in Mattawa that there isn't even a church.

Varied diet

But, you say, he speaks French.

Yes. And English. But, in his home, they speak only Russian. His wife was born in Danzig; however her native tongue is Russian and that is what the children speak when they come home from school.

On a special occasions, you won't find roast beef and Yorkshire pudding on the Monestime table. Nor is there fish every Friday. But you may find borscht and cabbage rolls and painted eggs.

I know. You think he caters to French Canadians and tells them they should be independent. (You think) politically he is Creditiste or Separatiste or spouts some other Quebec flavoured philosophy. (But no) Dr. Monestime is a Robarts' Conservative. He doesn't particularly like the Maple Leaf flag and says so. He feels too many Canadians are opposed to it for it to be embraced with the emotion a flag deserves.

So what is his secret?

"I told the people at the last election we should have better roads and better education. I would like to start a library-museum. I just want

to improve, improve, improve," he said.

All people understand that.

His four children were born in this country (No, he didn't cater to any group. The four are named Vala, Fedia, Yura and Sasha, hardly calculated to woo Mattawa ratepayers.)

He delivers babies and mends arms when kids fall out of trees and is ready to go anywhere - by helicopter sometimes - when a logger is injured in the bush. It doesn't matter whether the patient's name is Pierre or Eric or Hans or Singing Sky.

And the people of Mattawa understand that.

Humanitarian foundation

Sure there are some race differences, "but people are people," he explains. "This is a wonderful community. There is freedom, a sense of democracy, a good solid foundation of humanity."

The doctor has lived under dictators.

"Here there are many opinions," he says. "Under a dictator there is only one."

At 54 you might say that Dr. Firmin Monestime has learned what Canada is all about. He feels it in his bones. He knows the tears the widow sheds when she buries someone she loves in the Mattawa earth are not French or English, Catholic or Protestant, Socialist or conservative. They are just tears.

The most important human sound of all is a laugh. It, too, has no label, no nationality.

And Dr. Monestime laughs a lot.

You'd never guess over the telephone that he's Black.

-Reprinted with the permission of Gary's wife Jackie Lautens. Photo by Gary's son Richard Lautens.

and Bill Davis. He was also active during election campaigns supporting local Progressive Conservative Candidates. Conservative Minister of Finance Lorne Maeck visited Mattawa regularly at election time and on many other occasions supporting PC candidates and to deal with other issues. It helped that Dr. Monestime was a Conservative when dealing with town business with the Conservative government.

Lorne Maeck asked Dr. Monestime to nominate him in one election which was an indication of the appreciation of Dr. Monestime. Lorne Maeck tells about his visits to Mattawa with a smile. Everyone knew Dr. Monestime and he always drew enthusiastic crowds. He recalled one occasion when he was sick with a cold and Dr. Monestime gave him a needle and he felt better for the rest of the day's campaign. On another occasion Dr. Monestime told Mr. Maeck that he needed a fresh new blue tie and pulled him in to a local men's shop and bought him one.

Monestime Township

In October 1974 the Ontario Provincial Government decided to give some of the unorganized townships in Northern Ontario the names of deserving citizens and eliminate the established numbered method. Eleven people including Dr. Monestime were chosen and presented scrolls at a dinner hosted by MPP Lorne Maeck of South River. Monestime Township is

The 1975-76 Mattawa Town Council: (from top left) Clerk-Treasurer Louis Villeneuve, Councillors Paul Swindle, Fred Bangs, Ray Lavallee and Joe St. Eloi; (from bottom left) Councillor Mel Edwards, Mayor S. F. Monestime, Councillor Annie Lamont and Tax Collector Pierrette Burke.

The 1977-78 Mattawa Town Council: (from top left) Councillors Paul Swindle, Sid Turcotte, Acting Clerk-Treasurer Anne Desrochers, Councillor Fred Bangs and Deputy Mayor Mel Edwards; (from bottom left) Councillor Marjorie Wall, Mayor S. F. Monestime, and Councillor Annie Lamont.

Mayor Monestime accompanies Ontario Premier Bill Davis during a visit to a Mattawa school.

Mayor Monestime at a ceremony honouring Mattawa businessman and former Mayor Robert Ross (second left). With him are Councillor Annie Lamont and former Mayors Salem Turcotte (left) and Art Valois (right).

Mayor Monestime and wife Zena at party celebrating their 25 years in Mattawa.

Easy Rider

Mayor Monestime playing Donkey Baseball.

Mayor Monestime attends a graduation ceremony at the F.J. McElligot High School in Mattawa with Principal William J. Kennedy.

Mayor Monestime greets famous Mattawa speed walker, canoeist and logbuilder John Argo.

Zena Monestime (right) and her mother Valentina (left) enthusiastically supported Dr Monestime's political activities. Here they accompany Ontario Premier Bill Davis during a visit to Mattawa.

Ontario Premier Bill Davis is presented with a painting by Mattawa artist Gordon Dufoe (right). Presenting the painting are Lorne Maeck, Mayor Monestime and Councillor Annie Lamont.

in the Algoma District north of Manitoulin Island and can be seen on current maps. Coincidentally a small lake in the Township is called Russian Lake.

Another major project for Dr. Monestime the politician was a a run at federal Progressive Conservative politics.

Federal Politics

Dr. Monestime was active in the Mattawa Progressive Conservative Association before and after he became involved in local municipal politics. His experience in the Association was undoubtedly a factor in the development of his interest in local politics, with the support of his Association friends. Dr. Monestime was very supportive of the Mattawa PC Youth group. Philip "Ky" Turcotte, the President of the Youth group, has indicated that Dr. Monestime significantly and regularly

Mayor Monestime and Lorne Maeck the MPP for Parry Sound cut the ribbon to officially open the Laurentian Ski Club's new ski resort on Mount Antoine.

Progressive Conservative politicians greet the Ontario Municipal Affairs Minister Darcy McKeough in 1971. (From left) Parry Sound MPP Allister Johnston of South River. Mayor Monestime, Mr. McKeough and Mayor Merle Dickerson of North Bay.

John Diefenbaker greets Dr. Monestime after a meeting at the Royal York Hotel. Dr. Monestime admired John Diefenbaker particularly because he brought in the 1960 Canadian Bill of Rights.

encouraged the group. Philip became a youth representative in the national PC Association, and brought the local perspective to the federal table.

In 1967 Dr. Monestime considered running as a federal PC candidate during the brief period he was off the local municipal council and as his health improved. On one occasion he spoke to his friend John Diefenbaker while considering his decision to run. He eventually decided against it and was soon back in local politics again. Dr. Monestime continued to support federal and provincial PC candidates regularly during elections and at other times, by among other things speaking at their rallies. He eventually became a National Director of the Federal Progressive Conservative Party.

In another ground-breaking achievement he ran for the Presidency of the Federal Progressive Conservative party

Mattawa mayor may seek federal PC nomination

One candidate has indicated he is considering letting his name stand for the Progressive Conservative nomination in Nipissing for the Nov. 8 general election.

Dr. S. F. Monestime, mayor of Mattawa, was contacted by THE NUGGET this morning. He is recovering in the Toronto Orthopedic Hospital where he underwent surgery and bone graft on Friday. The doctor said he will await results of his operation to make a decision on his future political plans. He is expected to remain in hospital for another week.

But, Dr. Monestime indicated he is seriously considering running for the convention. He has previously indicated that his ambitions were in the federal field. From his hospital bed this week, he telephoned Opposition Leader John Diefenbaker who was in Toronto and discussed the election with the PC chief.

"I am under pressure for many parts to become a candidate in this election," stated the mayor of Mattawa. "I must admit I am seriously considering it and only the results of my operation may prevent me from seeking the Conservative ticket at the forthcoming convention."

Dr. Monestime indicated about a month ago that he will not be running for the office of mayor of Mattawa in the December municipal elections.

DR. S. F. MONESTIME

Dr. Monestime became well-known nearly two years ago as the first colored mayor in Ontario. He had been deputy mayor of Mattawa for one year before successfully seeking the office of mayor. He is a native of Haiti and was decorated by his native country for his work as a medical army officer during the Trujillo Massacre on the Dominican border.

Dr. Monestime is married to a Cazarist Russian and they have three children.

The date of the Progressive Conservative nomination convention has not yet beet set in Nipissing.

in 1971 and put on an active campaign before losing the vote. Many people supported him and he made several rousing speeches, extolling the importance of grassroots involvement in the party. Thirteen-year-old daughter Vala, who attended the event,

remembers vividly her father introducing Premier Bill Davis to her while Davis was meeting with her father in the hotel room.

Supporters wrote songs about him that they sang as they played accordion while marching through the Château Laurier Hotel in Ottawa. One, sung to the tune of This Land is Your Land, said: "Monestime is your Man/Monestime is our man/From Bonavista to Vancouver Island/From the Arctic Circle to the Great Lake Waters/Vote for this man to lead this land."

Besides continuing his medical practice, raising a family, acting as mayor, and running for PC president Dr. Monestime took on another major project, a nursing home for Mattawa.

WHERE RIVERS MEET

Federal Politics

Mattawa doctor seeks presidency of national PCs

S. FIRMIN MONESTIME, M.D.

NATIONAL DIRECTOR
PROGRESSIVE CONSERVATIVE PARTY OF CANADA
LE PARTI PROGRESSISTE CONSERVATEUR DU CANADA

MATTAWA, ONTARIO   TELEPHONE 744-5413

OTTAWA (CP) — Dr. Firman Monestime, mayor of Mattawa, Ont., has declared his candidacy for the presidency of the national Progressive Conservative party.

He now is a national director of the party and heads its local association in Mattawa, an Ottawa River community northwest of Ottawa.

He said in an interview Tuesday there is a need to stop confusion in the Conservatives' policy-making procedure.

That should be done by giving the Common premacy the help vice of at po

DR. S. F. MONESTIME

Dr. Monestime expresses his support for George Hees for leader of the PC party at the 1967 leadership Convention.

DR. MONESTIME FOR PRESIDENT

Badge worn by supporters at the 1971 convention.

Dr. Monestime speaks at the 1971 PC Convention.

Zena and Firmin

Zena and Firmin

Photo Album Two: Joie de Vivre

Firmin with Haitian singer Guy Durosier at Haitian Pavilion at Expo 67 in Montreal

Dancing with the children

Babie and Firmin

Relaxing after a hard day

Mattawa Old Home week

Firmin

Council meeting

With daughter Vala in 1967

Old Home week celebrations

Mattawa nursing home to have construction start in April

MATTAWA—Lucien Delean of the architects firm of Critchley and Delean of North Bay, has completed the final plan for Mattawa's new nursing home.

The nursing home is being established by the Algonquin Nursing Home, a private enterprise from Mattawa.

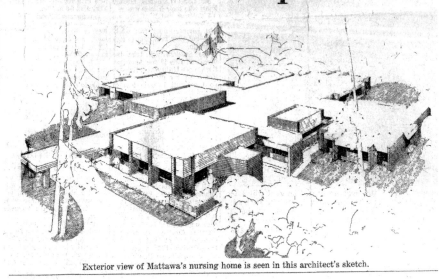

Exterior view of Mattawa's nursing home is seen in this architect's sketch.

Dr. Monestime (left) and MPP Lorne Maeck (right) greet Premier William Davis (centre) at the official opening of the Algonquin Nursing Home in 1976.

6
Triumph & Tragedy

"I was happy to have chosen Canada as my country. Being a physician, I devoted my life to helping people. Loving progress, I always fought for it and enjoyed being in politics to that end."- Dr. Monestime, 1977

THE YEAR 1976 brought into being one of Dr. Monestime's most lasting legacies and also brought great tragedy for the family and for Mattawa.

Algonquin Nursing Home

As a medical doctor and humanitarian Dr. Monestime as early as 1964 began to dream and talk about the need for a facility for the long term care of elderly people from Mattawa and area. It was devastating for the local elderly needing long term care to leave their community, their home, their family and friends in their final years.

Over the ensuing years Dr. Monestime had discussions with a group of doctors interested in a joint initiative, with companies that established homes for profit, with the Mattawa General Hospital and with his

A Place Called Home, the Algonquin Nursing Home.

municipal colleagues who supported the project. Dr. Monestime's persistence along with his entrepreneurial skills won over Ontario Premier Bill Davis. Community representatives Annie Lamont and Marjorie Wall from the Women's Institute accompanied Dr. Monestime on a trip to Toronto to formalize support. Pierrette Burke, Mattawa's secretary at the time, also went on the two day trip and took notes.

A November 1973 Mattawa council meeting was attended by Dr. Desmond Anthony a spokesman for the Upper Ottawa Valley Nursing Home group that was interested in possibly building a home. Dr. Monestime indicated that he was talking to the Laurentian Nursing Homes as a part of the process.

Dr. Monestime eventually personally established the Algonquin Nursing Home Limited (ANH) and submitted an excellent proposal for the home to the Ministry

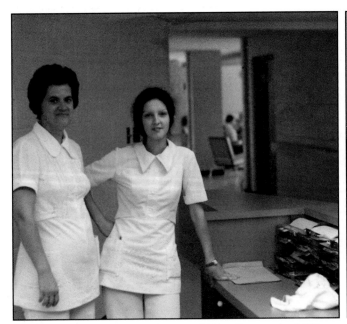

Nurse's Aides Irene Nadeau and Lise Breton in 1976.

Cooks Marie-Jeanne Amyotte and Cecile Johnson in the Algonquin Nursing Home dining room in 1976.

of Health. Property was purchased and an architectural plan sought.

The million dollar project between Ninth and Tenth Streets in Mattawa's Rosemount would have 60 beds and 14 staff including registered nurses. Semi-private and ward rooms were included with accommodations for couples.

There were many difficulties involved in getting the home going besides a monumental commitment in time and personal finance. He originally purchased a set of plans of another nursing home until he found they could not be used and had to sue a North Bay man to get his money back.

The Opening

The Algonquin Nursing Home opened on October 7th 1976 with Premier Bill Davis cutting the ribbon. Staffing and training soon fell into place and the Mattawa area had a long

term care home for its residents. Zena Monestime acted as Administrator.

Tragedy

1976 was a leap year which gave an extra day in February that the people of Mattawa wished had not happened. Fedia Monestime, the twenty-one-year-

Fedia Monestime around the time of his death in 1976.

old oldest Monestime son returned to Mattawa after a Saturday visit to a Deep River Carnival. He dropped in to the Trans-Canada Hotel around 12:30 am prior to heading home nearby. He noticed from a distance that there was an altercation between some of the town's young men and some men from Kitchener visiting the area. Both groups were significantly under the influence of a night's drinking. The visitors had been asked to leave the Valois Motel earlier and were now staying at the Mattawa House Hotel. No effort was made by Trans-Canada Hotel staff to stop the conflict and the police were not called to control the escalating confrontation.

Ralph Donald Childerhose of Kitchener panicked and ran to his car and grabbed his .22 calibre semi-automatic rifle and fired three shots into the walls of the hotel, presumably to scare off the Mattawa men giving his friends a hard time, and ran and hid.

WHERE RIVERS MEET

Kitchener man charged with non-capital murder

Mattawa mayor's son dead, 3 injured in shootings

(See pictures on page 2)

By GORDON McCULLOCH
Nugget Temiscaming-
Mattawa Bureau

MATTAWA—One man is dead, one is in serious condition and two are suffering leg wounds following a shooting incident here early Sunday morning.

Dead is Fedia Monestime, 21, son of Mattawa's mayor, Dr. S. F. Monestime.

In serious condition at North Bay Civic Hospital is Edmund Ladouceur, 40, of Mattawa. When admitted, his condition was listed as critical.

Also in Civic Hospital are Danny Decaire and James Pedersen, both 19, of Mattawa each suffering a gunshot wound to their right legs.

In custody and charged with non-capital murder is Ralph Donald Childerhose, 29, of 167 Morgan Ave., Kitchener, Ont. Childerhose appeared before Justice of the Peace Louis Villeneuve and was taken to the District Jail at North Bay. He was remanded until March 5 when he will appear in Provincial Court at North Bay.

OPP said the shooting arose from a fight that began in the Trans-Canada Hotel involving four men from the Cambridge, Ont. area, who were visiting here, and a group of local men.

One of the visitors was badly beaten about the face and suffered a broken nose. One of his companions went to a van parked on the street outside the hotel and returned to the doorway of the hotel lounge with a semi-automatic .22 calibre rifle.

He fired three shots into the wall of the building.

From information given to police, there were exclamations of "they're just blanks."

The man ran into the street followed by a crowd from the hotel. Once outside, he turned and fired among his pursuers, striking four persons, OPP said.

When members of the Mattawa OPP detachment arrived at the scene, three men were

FEDIA MONESTIME

lying in the street and one was being supported by a friend.

All four wounded were taken to the Mattawa General Hospital for treatment and transferred to the Civic Hospital at North Bay.

Fedia Monestime was pronounced dead on arrival at North Bay.

About 1.31 a.m., the suspect was taken into custody by Mattawa OPP.

All four of the visitors were questioned by the police but only the suspect was detained.

Constables from the North Bay OPP detachment were called to the scene along with OPP Detective Sgt. Jim Harrod and Const. John Mash of the OPP identification unit, District 12 headquarters.

Detective Inspector Tom Hill of the OPP Criminal Investigation Department, Toronto, was also called to Mattawa.

Const. L. W. Goodkey of the Mattawa OPP and Det. Sgt. Harrod conducted the investigation.

From early morning until about 1.35 p.m. the section of Main St. from Bangs to McConnell Sts. to McConnell St., were cordoned by the police.

Eyewitnesses to the incident, interviewed by The Nugget, were reluctant to talk about the episode and it seemed they

wanted to believe it never happened.

One eyewitness said he heard gunshots and saw people fall in the street, but the "whole scene seemed unreal," he said.

Some related what they had seen but said they preferred to remain anonymous.

* * * *

Most of the citizens approached seemed to be shocked by the fact that an incident of this kind could happen in a town like Mattawa.

A taxi driver said he saw a man come from the hotel into the street and raise a rifle but

* * * *

Doctor treats dying son

MATTAWA (Staff)—Pathos was added to tragedy in the shooting incident here early Sunday morning, when Dr. S. F. Monestime, who was on medical alert at the time, was called to treat the four wounded men, not knowing that one of them was his own son.

Dr. Monestime told The Nugget that he only recognized one of the injured men as his son when he attempted to treat him.

He called the young man's name, and although his son momentarily opened his eyes, he didn't speak and according to the doctor, his son lapsed into a state of shock.

"I knew he was going to die but I had no alternative than to send him to North Bay by ambulance," said Dr. Monestime.

According to Dr. Monestime, his son had told a nurse at the Mattawa General Hospital, when he was first brought in for

treatment, that he was not seriously injured and felt no pain.

The doctor said there was a small wound on the lower right side of his son's abdomen where the bullet had entered. There was little exterior bleeding. He believed the projectile must have severed an artery and internal bleeding quickly brought on a state of shock.

Dr. Monestime and his wife accompanied their injured son in the ambulance to North Bay Civic Hospital.

"The boy died on the way," he said.

The doctor had only praise for the reception at the North Bay hospital where, he said, four doctors were waiting.

"I have been 40 years a physician and 25 years in Mattawa. During that time I have always tried to help people but I couldn't help my own son," said the doctor, obviously

the cab-driver didn't wait to see what happened.

There was a general feeling of hostility for what was termed a "senseless tragedy."

Many expressed the hope that the new firearms regulations proposed by the government, would soon be implemented.

* * * *

shaken by the death of his eldest son.

"All I can say now is that I want to see justice done."

Just prior to his death, the young man had been studying business administration at Canadore College, North Bay. He was expected to take a position in the Algonquin Nursing Home at Mattawa, upon completion of his studies.

He is survived by his parents, his maternal grandmother, two sisters, Valentina, 22, now attending Ottawa University; Sasha, 12, at home and a brother, Yura, 14, also at home.

Deputy-Mayor Mel Edwards expressed, on behalf of the Mattawa Town Council, "deep

sympathy for the Monestime family."

He also said that Mayor Merle Dickerson of North Bay had personally conveyed to him the "expressions of regret on behalf of the members of the North Bay City Council."

Funeral services will be held on Wednesday at Mattawa.

Arrangements are being made through the McGuinty Funeral Home, North Bay.

Fedia will be resting at the Monestime residence after 1 p.m. Tuesday.

Interment will be at Mattawa.

Part of Mattawa's Main St. is cordoned by the OPP during the investigation.

* * * *   * * * *   * * * *

Scenes at Mattawa shootings

This photograph shows the van from which the semi-automatic .22 calibre rifle was taken at the scene of the shooting. The dark spot at bottom right of the steps is a blood stain on the snow. One of the victims collapsed at this point. The four victims were shot in front of this restaurant.
—Nugget Staff Photos by Gordon McCulloch

News reports of the death and funeral of Fedia Monestime. Below is the telegram sent by former Canadian Prime Minister John Diefenbaker on news of Dr. Monestime's loss.

Rev. Vladimir Malchenko, assistant pastor of the Russian Orthodox Church, Toronto, leads the pallbearers from St. Anne's Roman Catholic Church, Mattawa, as they carry the body of Fedia Monestime, 21, shooting victim and son of Dr. and Mrs. S. F. Monestime.
—Nugget Staff Photo by Gordon McCulloch

* * * *   * * * *   * * * *   * * * *

Hundreds pay final tribute to Mattawa shooting victim

By GORDON McCULLOCH
Nugget Temiscaming-
Mattawa Bureau

MATTAWA—Hundreds of citizens paid final tribute on Wednesday to Fedia Monestime, 21, who died as a result of a shooting incident early Sunday morning. The young man was the son of Mattawa's mayor, Dr. S. F. Monestime.

There was an unbroken line of

vehicles extending from the Monestime residence on Pembroke Rd., where the body had been resting, to St. Anne's Roman Catholic Church in Rosemount, as the funeral cortege moved through the main thoroughfare.

Within the church there was standing room only.

Rev. Dimitri Sever, director of the Protection of the Holy Virgin Russian Orthodox Church, Ottawa, and Rev.

Vladimir Malchenko, assistant pastor of the Russian Orthodox Church, Toronto officiated.

Members of the Mattawa Town Council attended as a group.

An honor guard comprised of members of the Mattawa Cadet Corps No. 2442 under the command of Capt. Arthur Davis, CD, was present.

Guard members included: Cadet Lt. Steve Montgomery, Cadet Sgt. Richard Gravelle, Cadet Sgt. Angela Bangs, Cadet Cpl. Lena Michaud and Cadets Madeleine Saari and Paul Viel.

Fedia Monestime had been a leader in the Mattawa Cadet Corps and in 1970 had been winner of the best cadet of the company award, at a leadership course at Vernon, B.C.

Cemetery and the funeral arrangements were under the direction of the McGuinty Funeral Home, North Bay.

Fedia Monestime is survived by his parents, his maternal grandmother, Valentina Petschersky, a sister Vala, 22, now attending the University of Ottawa; and two brothers, Yura, 14 and Sasha, 12.

THREE WOUNDED

Three other men were wounded in the Sunday shooting. Edmund Ladouceur, 40, of Mattawa is in North Bay Civic Hospital in "fair" condition after suffering a gunshot wound to the throat.

Danny Decaire, 19, and Jim Pedersen, 19, both of Mattawa, are also in hospital in "satisfactory" condition, each

ZCZC MDP007 021150

FPB589

GGBO60 FR OTTAWA ONT 2-3 1138A EST

HIS WORSHIP MAYOR DR F.S. MONESTIME,

MATTAWA ONTARIO

BT

OLIVE AND EXTEND TO YOU AND YOURS OUR DEEPEST SYMPATHY IN THE

TRAGIC PASSING OF YOUR SON. OUR HEARTS AND THOUGHTS ARE WITH

YOU.

JOHN DIEFENBAKER

TRIUMPH AND TRAGEDY

59

Patrons filed on to the street and Childerhose began to randomly fire again. Danny Decaire and Jim Pederson both nineteen were shot in the leg and Raymond Ladoucer, forty, was also hit. Fedia was shot in the stomach and fell in front of the restaurant next door where he was going to call police (coincidentally this was the former location of the Chez Francois restaurant). All of the men were rushed to the hospital.

Dr. Monestime, who was on-call that evening, received a call at home about the shootings and was told to come to the hospital. Much to his surprise he was also told to bring Zena. They rushed to the hospital. When they arrived they where told that Fedia was one of the victims. They went to Fedia's bedside and called his name. He opened his eyes briefly and lapsed into unconsciousness. The bullet had severed an artery causing internal bleeding. He never regained consciousness.

News reports the next day called Fedia "one of the town's most popular men." He attended St. Anne's Separate School and F.J. McElligott Secondary School where he was an excellent athlete. He had completed a year at Canadore College and intended to return to study administration to help at the family's new Algonquin Nursing Home. He had been a Scout for years and had won an award as the best cadet in a Canadian Cadet Corps event in British Columbia.

Condolences poured in to the Monestime family including one from former Prime Minister John

Diefenbaker and other Members of Parliament. A huge funeral cortege ran through town from the Monestime home to St. Anne's Roman Catholic Church. Within the church there was standing room only. The family is Russian Orthodox and priests from Ottawa and Toronto conducted the ceremony. Other Mattawa clergy attended. There was an honour guard by the Canadian Cadet Corp. Groups of elementary and secondary school students attended. In Russian Orthodox tradition everyone stood during the two hour ceremony and everyone filed past the open casket.

The Aftermath

The town was shocked and angry at the tragedy and by the lawlessness of a few in the town and especially at the hotel. A town meeting of over 250 people met to discuss appropriate action. Dr. Monestime expressed his feelings as Fedia's father and as mayor of Mattawa. There was talk of stronger policing and more activities for young people. In October a municipal by-law was passed making it illegal for anyone under the age of 16 to be on the streets of Mattawa after 9 p.m. unless accompanied by someone over 18. The OPP would enforce the by-law and assign fines.

The Childerhose Trial

Ralph Donald Childerhose was taken into custody shortly after the February 29 shootings and charged with non-capital

After Ralph Donald Childerhose was acquitted in Fedia's death, Dr. Monestime fought for an appeal but was unsuccessful. He contacted the Attorney General and Members of Parliament to no avail. The Town Council passed bylaws to curb the drinking and violence.

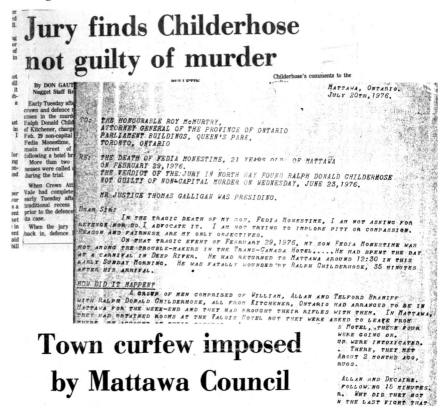

Jury finds Childerhose not guilty of murder

Town curfew imposed by Mattawa Council

murder. The two young men who were shot improved quickly with no long term effects. Mr. Ladoucer was in serious condition but survived.

Childerhose went to trial on June 23, 1976. In simple terms it was stated that the Kitchener men were in Mattawa for the weekend and had been drinking and visiting various pubs. They came to the Trans-Canada Hotel after midnight on the night of the incident. A fight broke out with some Mattawa youth and one of the Kitchener men was hurt. The hotel management took no action. Childerhose went to his car and brought in the gun and fired three shots into the hotel walls and ran out.

Edmund Ladoucer left to go home nearby and was shot. Fedia Monestime went to the restaurant next door for help and was also shot. Evidence was presented that Childerhose was pursued but this was contradicted with indications that he had hidden in the dark and ambushed the victims. It was made clear by the OPP that Fedia was an innocent bystander.

Childerhose's lawyer argued self-defence. The jury found Childerhose not guilty and he was set free.

The citizens of Mattawa were in shock. Dr. Monestime fought for an appeal but was unsuccessful. He contacted the Attorney General and Members of Parliament to no avail. Coincidentally there was a major debate about capital punishment at the time and it was abolished with many people still wanting

Dr. S. F. Monestime, guest of honor at a testimonial dinner sponsored by the citizens of Mattawa, cuts the cake symbolizing his 25 years of dedication to the community. Guests were, from left, Fern Duhaime, Mrs. Monestime, Mike Finner, Mrs. Maeck, Dr. Monestime, Lorne Maeck, MPP for Parry Sound, Councillor Annie Lamont, Mrs. Hopkins and Len Hopkins, MP for Renfrew North-Nipissing East.
—Nugget Staff Photo

Mattawa mayor honored for 25 years in community

harsh punishment for offenders—while at the same time Childerhose was set free. It had devastating impact on Dr. Monestime's emotional health but he kept on with his medical practice, his duties as the mayor and his successful efforts to open the Algonquin Nursing Home. The family and the community mourned the death and were hurt by the injustice they perceived in the case.

Testimonial Dinner

On August 30, 1976 Some 300 Mattawa residents gathered in a surprise event to honour Dr. Monestime for his 25 years of service to Mattawa as a doctor and politician. Mike Finner was Master of Ceremonies for the event at the Mattawa Community Centre. Mrs. Fern Duhaime took the lead in developing and sponsoring the event.

In his remarks Mr. Finner

This photograph of Dr. S. F. Monestime, taken near the end of his career, is hanging in the Algonquin Nursing Home. A copy will be put in the new Dr. S. F. Monestime Council Chambers in 2009.

noted that Dr. Monestime was a doctor who made many house calls for the convenience of his patients. MP Len Hopkins and MPP Lorne Maeck made presentations to Dr. Monestime. Mrs. Duhaime and Fred Bangs presented gifts from the community and Annie Lamont presented a citation prepared by the Sisters at the Mattawa General Hospital.

Dr. Monestime thanked the people for accepting him and his family so generously in to their hearts and called Mattawa "a little heaven." He made special reference to the people who went out of their way to help him in 1951 when he set up practice in Mattawa.

Illness

By the end of 1976 Dr. Monestime was exhausted from the stress around the death of his son Fedia and the struggle to open the nursing home.

He was also stressed by arbitrated high union wages due to inflation at the time. Fortunately Prime Minister Pierre Trudeau brought in anti-inflation legislation which temporarily rolled back wages.

On December 31, 1976 he officially terminated his medical career after close to 40 years of intense involvement in the profession. He continued his duties as mayor.

A letter from a travel agency outlined a two week Caribbean vacation including his first return visit to Haiti. He then realized his health was failing and the trip was cancelled. He eventually spent a month in the

DR. S. F. MONESTIME

⁎ ⁎ ⁎   ⁎ ⁎ ⁎

First black mayor, Dr. Monestime dies in Mattawa

Announcement in the *North Bay Nugget* of the death of Dr. Monestime.

Royal Victoria Hospital in Montreal where he was operated on for pancreatic cancer.

While at the hospital on October 3, 1977, he wrote a sad note to the people of Mattawa:

Au Revoir. I was happy to have chosen Canada as my country. Being a physician, I devoted my life to helping people. Loving progress, I always fought for it and enjoyed being in politics to that end.

But 'le destin' of my son in February 1976 and the remaining injustice and

another blow in February 1977 which was given to me at the nursing home I had planned for so many years and fought so hard to build for the people of Mattawa, all this has broken my will to live and fight."

He returned to the Mattawa General Hospital from Montreal and died on October 27th, 1977 at age 67.

Funeral services were held at the St. Anne's Roman Catholic Church in Mattawa and were conducted according to the rites of the Russian Orthodox Church.

North Bay Nugget reporter Gordon McCulloch wrote that: "Mattawa's traditional smiling face was somber Monday.

Residents of the town and area, municipal officials of the district, parliamentary representatives from both provincial and federal levels, dignitaries from Ontario and Quebec along with friends and relatives, gathered here to pay a final tribute to Dr. Saint Firmin Monestime, Mayor of Mattawa, who died Thursday. In respect for the memory of the man who had been involved in the destiny of the town and who had been part of the medical fraternity of Mattawa since 1951, all places of business and all schools in the town, were closed during the day.

Relatives and friends from Haiti were present at the Monday services. Members of the Mattawa Town Council, mayors and reeves from neighbouring municipalities, members of the Mattawa Volunteer Fire

Brigade, the Mattawa Cadet Corps, staff members and nurses from the Mattawa General Hospital and the Algonquin Nursing Home, formed an honour guard at St. Anne's Church. Representatives of the medical fraternity from Mattawa, North Bay, Ottawa and Montreal were also present. Lorne Maeck, MPP for Parry Sound, a personal friend of Dr. Monestime attended.

Active pallbearers were Denis Turcotte, Jean-Marc Morin, Larry Bangs, Mauril Belanger, Mike Finner, Phillip Turcotte. Honorary pallbearers included Roma Julien, Lucien Duquette, Albert Morin, Joseph Montreuil, William Sanderson, Norman Mann, Francois Martin, Ernest Simpson, Joe St. Eloi, Albert Hurdman, Adelard Belanger and Arthur Valois Jr."

McCulloch then recounted a short history of Dr. Monestime's political career and concluded by writing that everyone agreed that the "memory of the man would not easily be forgotten and wherever the townspeople of Mattawa should meet, Firmin Monestime would always be a popular and welcome subject of conversation."

Rev. Dimitri Sever, left, director, and Canon Theodore Sever, of the Russian Orthodox Church, Ottawa, lead the procession as the body of Dr. Firmin Monestime, Mayor of Mattawa, is carried from St. Anne Roman Catholic Church, Mattawa, following the funeral ceremonies Monday.

—Nugget Staff Photo

★ ★ ★   ★ ★ ★   ★ ★ ★

People of all walks of life pay tribute to memory of Mattawa's Dr. Monestime

By GORDON McCULLOCH
Nugget District Editor
MATTAWA — Mattawa's traditional smiling face was sombre Monday.

Residents of the town and area, municipal officials of the district, parliamentary representatives from both provincial and federal levels,

Canada, Felipe Contave along with many Canadian parliamentary dignitaries, expected to be present for the funeral, were unable to attend.

Members of the Mattawa Town Council, mayors and reeves from neighboring municipalities, members of the Mattawa Volunteer Fire

blackout and delivery was performed with the aid of portable lights.

Dr. Monestime spent a year of post-graduate studies in Edinburgh, Scotland.

His political career began in 1962 when he was elected to the Mattawa Town Council. The following year he became

Zena Monestime (EE)

7
Legacy & Recognition

"The secret to my husband's success in life was that all people were equal in his eyes."- Zena Monestime, 2003

Besides being the first Black mayor in Canada Dr. Monestime and his family have left and are leaving a lasting legacy in Mattawa and Area.

Algonquin Nursing Home

When Dr. Monestime died just a year after the opening of the Algonquin Nursing Home many decisions had to be made. Individual and company offers of purchase were forthcoming, some even before his death. The decision was to wait

Algonquin Nursing Home advertisement celebrating the 100th anniversary of Mattawa in 1984.

and see and his wife Zena continued her role as Administrator with full support of her family, staff, and residents. It was eventually decided to keep the home in the family. Daughter Vala joined her mother in the spring of 1978 as Director of Nursing. She had graduated with a Bachelor of Science in Nursing from the University of Ottawa.

With outstanding leadership, staff, and support the facility soon filled and began its outstanding work. Many improvements were made in services and programming and many volunteers were recruited. In

WELCOME TO MATTAWA

The Algonquin Nursing Home is proud to be part of Mattawa's Centennial Year. The administrator, residents and staff welcome all visitors to Mattawa and invite everyone to visit us, especially during Homecoming Week.

In April, 1976, a modern one-storey, 60-bed extended care nursing home was opened by the late Dr. S. F. Monestime in a residential area of Mattawa. In 1984, five new bedrooms were added to the center wing, along with a chapel, a second lounge, a physiotherapy room and a larger activity room. The home is accredited and licensed by the Ministry of Health and is an active member of the Ontario Nursing Home Association. The care provided is supervised by registered staff 24 hours a day. Excellent medical care is available from three local physicians. The medical and nursing care, together with a qualified Activity Director and a qualified Food Service Supervisor, kitchen, housekeeping and laundry staff, ensure your physical, mental and social well-being. Private and semi-private rooms, including accommodations for couples, are available. Friends can visit anytime and residents may go out overnight or on weekends with the doctor's permission.

ALGONQUIN NURSING HOME

Ninth Street, Mattawa, Ontario
744-2202

Administrator: Mrs. Z. Monestime

1985 the Honourable Alan Pope, Minister of Health and the Honourable Ernie Eves, local MPP, and Minister of Skills Development officially opened a new addition. It provided a larger living area, a new chapel, 12 extended care beds, a second dining room and the capacity was raised to 72.

In 1992 the home received official designation under the French Languages Act. Some staff received language training and there were improved transfer payments to support the initiative. Since 1981 the home has regularly received accreditation indicating the meeting of the highest standards of the Canadian Council of Accreditation.

The home's success also depended on the hard work and commitment of the staff who worked there over the years, some of whom had lengthy careers going back to the opening.

Zena

Beside the remarkable achievement of Dr. Monestime there is no question that the accomplishments of Zena in surviving the deaths of her husband and son Fedia and taking charge of the development of the nursing home are monumental achievements. Her combination of incredible nurturing and organizational skills, balanced with the occasional necessity for toughness, allowed her to develop and administer the Nursing Home for some twenty-five years. With Valentina at home until her death in 1995 and daughter Vala at her side, hard-work paid dividends in one of Mattawa's truly outstanding

Mattawa nursing home receives accreditation

Many articles on the Algonquin Nursing Home have appeared in the *North Bay Nugget* and the local newspaper *The Mattawa Recorder* over the years.

Staff meetings at the Algonquin Nursing Home, Mattawa, are orderly but informal. From left: Vala Monestime-Belter, director of nursing; Zena Monestime, administrator and wife of the founder of the home the late Dr. S. F. Monestime; Gail Peplinskie, head nurse; Helen Coutu, secretary and Pauline Laundriault, activity director.
Nugget Staff Photo

By GORD McCULLOCH
Temiscaming-Mattawa Bureau

MATTAWA — The Algonquin Nursing Home has been officially awarded status of accreditation by the Canadian Council on Hospital Accreditation.

According to the document acknowledging the fact, the Mattawa home has achieved "standards for quality of care set by council and achieved through the combined efforts of the governing body and management, the professional and supporting staffs with voluntary assistance from the residents of the community."

"We have worked towards this since 1981 and now an unbiased group, experienced in all branches of health care, has given us status," said Vala Monestime-Belter, director of nursing at Algonquin Nursing Home.

"It means we have met and surpassed all standards set for nursing homes. We are in top shape and proud of it," said Pauline Laundriault, activity director for the home.

Head nurse Gail Peplinskie and secretary Helen Coutu also expressed pride in the new status acquired by the home. "Everyone feels good about this, but it doesn't mean we can stop working towards greater improvements," said Zena Monestime, home administrator.

The Algonquin Nursing Home was established

Gord McCulloch, The Nugget

Zena Monestime, seated, owner and administrator of Algonquin Nursing Home, discusses new bilingual certificate with staffers Vala Monestime, left, and Pauline Landriault.

Home, hospital now bilingual

N 0 2 1992

tawa has d a bilin-

stitutions, Home and Hospital, ted bilin-ench-Lan-

ill 8, was

tor of the Mattawa General Hospital.

Speakers at the nursing home included Mrs. Monestime and several staffers; Mattawa Mayor Colette Wilson; and Father Basil Tanguay of St. Anne's Parish.

Joining them were Dr. Catherine Whiting of the district health council; Dr. Jean-Marie Rochefort, Monique Mechefske, and Gilles Huot, representing French-language health services;

and home residents Yolande Belanger, Roger Labelle, and Arneault Laperle.

"In 1976 when my husband built this facility, he provided the foundation to ensure adequate availability of French-language services. The French-language implementation plan has formalized and expanded on his foundation. Here at the home we consider speaking French to our residents as part of the care we provide for

LIZ

Zena Monestime, Sacha Belter, 8, his mother Vala Belter, and Marjorie Wall share a conversation outside the Algonquin Nu Mattawa Wednesday. The home is planning an expansion to its di ing room and staff room.

heating system will be changed from electric to gas.

"The new heating will allow us to provide a moister heat. Electric tends to dry the skin in winter," said Belter.

Monestime said the expansion is a wise business decision.

"We are proud of our reputation across the province," she said.

"We get residents from Toronto,

but more offer their servic Lise Rozon, are available day or night.

"It's nothing to call Lis have her be with someone said Belter.

The nursing home is al all the schools in the town centre.

"It really is magical th

New Entrance Open at Algonquin Nursing Home

Mrs. M sits with "Tiger" and enjoys a visit with Violet Alan (left), Elizabeth Commando and Eileen Label (right) in the new foyer.
Photo by Sue Bruemmer

WHERE RIVERS MEET

Yura (left) and Sasha (right) Monestime with their mother Zena and grandmother Valentina. Valentina died in 1995 and Zena in 2005.

The Polyanka Russian Dancers perform on the stage in front of the Mattawa & District Museum.

achievements. Zena Monestime became ill in 2003 and died in 2005. Her daughter Vala Monestime Belter became Administrator

Improvements were made recently to the grounds to encourage more outdoor activity. With 73 beds and about 86 staff the Algonquin Nursing Home has become a model for long term care and the largest employer and tax payer in Mattawa. Hundreds of Mattawa and area elderly have been well served by the home over the years.

The home is recognized as Dr. Monestime's greatest individual achievement and serves as an ongoing memorial to the present day to his remarkable insight and initiative and to the subsequent leadership of his wife Zena and daughter Vala.

The Monestime family remains close to the present day, meets regularly, and attends Russian Orthodox services on occasion.

Vala is married to Wayne Belter, Mattawa's Administrator-Clerk-Treasurer, and they have three children: Katya (24), Sasha (21), and Misha (19) who are all in university and have done extensive community volunteer work.

Vala's brother Sasha is raising his family in southern Ontario. He is married to Sharon Amadeo and they have four children: Nikolai (17), Tatyana (15), Natalya (12), and Adriana (10).

Brother Yura is married to Cindy Boston. After 25 years in television and video production covering national, international and local events, Yura is teaching television production at North Bay's Canadore College.

Russian Heritage

Zena Monestime, her mother Valentina and daughter Vala,

Part of the Russian Heritage Exhibit at the Mattawa & District Museum.

The Monestime extended family remains close to the present day. (Back row L to R) Wayne Belter, Sasha Belter, Vala Monestime Belter, Katya Belter, Misha Belter, Cindy Boston, Tatyana Monestime, Nikolai Monestime, Sharon Monestime, Sasha Monestime and Yura Monestime. (Front row L to R) Natalya Monestime and Adriana Monestime.

along with other volunteers, presented an exhibition of Russian-Canadian archival material at the Mattawa Museum from August 9-16th 1986, as a part of the Mattawa Summer Festival.

A large display of heirloom pieces - coins, medals, embroideries, books, photographs, figurines, etc. were on display for the week. Videos on Russian topics of interest ran throughout the week. The Polyanka Russian Dancers performed on the stage at the Museum at a Sunday event. As a follow up to this event the Mattawa Museum also has a display of Russian heritage donated by the family.

Haitian Relatives

It appears that Dr. Monestime's Haitian relatives had some knowledge of his progress and success in Canada.

Dr. Monestime received a letter of congratulations from Haiti on becoming mayor. The letter from the "Club La Jeunesse" complimented Dr. Monestime on his achievement and mentioned that the Secretary General of the club was his son Daniel. It also mentioned with pleasure that his victory was a compliment to the small country of Haiti. They stated: "We are certain that you will not fail to uphold this excellent choice of the people."

Daniel now lives in Montreal and visits Haiti regularly. Daniel has four sons and three daughters. Daughter Daniella lives in Ottawa. She admires her grandfather. Dr. Monestime's daughter Eddie married and has five children.

Haitian family members attended the funerals of Fedia and Dr. Monestime.

Dr. Monestime's full life and gravitation to the Russian side of his marriage did not allow for the nurturing of his Haitian connections. There is no indication that he regretted his Haitian past. He visited and corresponded regularly with Haitian friends in Canada including Dr. Hypolyte and Dr. Wiss who practiced in Sudbury. As mentioned, he maintained contact with his friend, Haitian historian Laurore St-Juste. Indeed he was scheduled to visit Haiti in 1977 when he became ill and cancelled the trip.

Mattawa Museum Exhibit

In August 2004 some 27 years after Dr. Monestime's death, family and friends

A display case full of family artifacts is part of the Dr. S. F. Monestime exhibit at the Mattawa & District Museum.

remembered his contribution and powerful presence. His family authorized a display of artifacts, photographs, written material and a short movie presentation for a display at the Mattawa and District Museum.

Mike Finner the retired teacher who was the M.C. at the 25th Anniversary party for Dr. Monestime in 1976 acted as M.C. of the opening of the exhibit. There were many glowing remarks from the large gathering, some of which were repeated in the *Mattawa Recorder* and the *North Bay Nugget*.

Vala Monestime Belter commented: "We are so very pleased to gather tonight in honour of my father. His influence on his community and his family continues to this day and is evidenced by this turnout 27 years after his death. He came from the small French Caribbean island country of Haiti—a land of sunshine and bananas, where

people dance to calypso-type music, to a land of snow and black flies, filled with white people who spoke a different language and shivered in winter. Even though already a doctor in Haiti with several published books, my father returned to school in Quebec in order to be

able to practice in Canada. Dad then embraced the Russian culture and religion of the lady he married. He loved progress. From street signs and sewers, from housing projects to paved roads and street lights, from the seniors' centre to Mattawa's very own seniors' home, Dad saw the

Guests Sue Lamirante, Rose Simpson and Marilyn Gauthier look at the video presentation at the Dr. S. F. Monestime exhibit.

Remarks by Zena Monestime at her husband's Museum Exhibit Opening

I am honoured that so many accepted our invitation to celebrate the life of Mattawa's friend, doctor, mayor, politician and my husband, Saint Firmin Monestime. He adopted Canada as his country and fate brought him to Mattawa. He fell in love with its beauty and its people. As a physician, he was never too tired, even in thirty below weather, to make a house call, to fly into the bush to mend a broken leg, to deliver so many of Mattawa's babies, and so many I see here tonight.

In between performing surgeries of all kinds, there was always time to listen to people's problems and try to help. He shared in your sad times, and was very happy to enjoy the good times as well. Not to mention on many occasions a good steak with a rum and coke in your homes. My husband was a wonderful father to his four children. He instilled in them the values and morals he deeply believed in. He adored his mother-in-law, Valentina Petschersky, who lived with us. He especially loved her cooking. For that I am thankful because I must confess, cooking was not one of his wife's best qualities.

Zena (right) greets Mme Yolande Belanger at the exhibit honouring Dr. Monestime.

Being a man of vision, he worked hard as councillor and mayor to make Mattawa a better place. And I am quite proud when I recall the world coverage when he became North America's first coloured mayor. I loved his varied interests, his knowledge of history, literature, world events and politics. He loved learning. After retiring as a doctor, his dream was to return to school to study law.

The secret to my husband's success in life was that all people were equal in his eyes. There's a lot more that I would like to say, but then again you knew him too.

Thank you to all the speakers. I know why my husband thought so well of you. And thanks to all who have joined us this evening to honour his memory.

Thank you…

---

potential in everything and everyone. In the days, when people fought over civil rights in United States, he was elected the first Black mayor in North America. There was international acclaim for him and for Mattawa as this opened doors for others to also have equal opportunity in life. I've never figured out if my father chose Mattawa or if Mattawa chose him - undoubtedly both. You adopted the French-speaking Haitian who chose to become a Canadian. You shared your family gatherings, your troubles, your good times, your cigarettes and your laughter. I would like to thank you for giving him your friendship."

Vala Monestime Belter also spoke about her mother Zena who played such an important part in their family life. Vala said: "Although tonight is about my father, it is also of course about my mother. My Dad not only saw her beauty, but her love of family, her loyalty, her strength of character and strong convictions. She had faith in him and gave him the courage and support he needed. To this day she ensures that the dream they shared continues in The Algonquin Nursing Home, with love and respect. Daily, she shows her children, grandchildren, friends and staff, that life must be met head on, but with dignity and grace."

Zena Monestime also spoke. (see sidebar above)

Jean Marc Morin, whose parents knew Dr. Monestime well, also spoke. Dr. Monestime visited them regularly and often stayed late into the night. Dr. Monestime took their young and restless son Marc under wing and Marc became a friend and chauffeur to Dr. Monestime getting to know him better than many as they travelled to many events. Dr. Monestime was a remarkable story teller and conversationalist and a great listener on these occasions.

Marc asked his family for their comments and they said what many others have said. His sister said: "He always took the time to listen and talk with me. I trusted him and did not want to disappoint him. He provided

Greetings from Liberal MP
Mauril Belanger

In the early 1970s Mattawa student Mauril Belanger, now a five time Liberal MP for Ottawa Vanier in the federal legislature, knew Dr. Monestime well. As a nineteen-year old high school student, Mauril and a friend created a summer employment program for pre-teens in Mattawa by applying for a grant to support the project. The object was to take the pre-teens to the nearby Antoine Provincial Park for week long programs of intense recreational activity. Dr. Monestime was very supportive and wrote a letter of recommendation to help get the grant. Mauril knew Dr. Monestime in his university years when he was President of the Student's Federation at the University of Ottawa. He later remembered how unique it was to have a Black man with a deep voice and infectious laugh as mayor

Mauril has had many important roles as a MP including a cabinet post and was Deputy Clerk of the government in the House of Commons, as well as Minister of

Internal Trade. One of his roles was co-chair of the Canadian African Parliamentary Group, where he was very aware of Black history and spoke of Dr. Monestime to people in Haiti on occasion during his four visits there over the years. Mauril and his family were very supportive of Dr. Monestime and saw nothing out of the ordinary in him being the mayor of Mattawa for years. Mauril was a pallbearer at Dr. Monestime's funeral.

The following are remarks sent by Mauril Belanger to the opening of

the Museum Display on Dr. Monestime in 2004:

"Saint-Firmin était un home remarquable et remarqué. Que ce soit en tant que père de famille, conjoint, médecin, nouveau citoyen ou maire de Mattawa, il a toujours sut se dépasser et entraîner les autres dans son sillon.

I remember him proudly as a friend of the family and an able politician who navigated adroitly in the sometimes-tricky waters of partisan politics.

All who knew him are thankful for having known him, for having shared his contagious laughter and for having experienced first hand his love for his fellow human beings.

Saint-Firmin était de plusieurs façons le précurseur de ce que devient le Canada; une terre d'accueil qui sait faire une place sous le soleil pour toutes les cultures du monde.

My congratulations and thanks to the Mattawa & District Museum and its directors for this initiative."

---

guidance and encouragement and was quick to praise. I loved his laugh. I loved him as much as one person can love another without being in love."

Jack Whalen one of Mattawa's local historians, a retired teacher, and former councillor with Dr. Monestime and a friend told a story of Dr. Monestime and his role in Mattawa's wide spread recognition. He said: "What is important to note is that everywhere Dr. Monestime went and in everything that he did, he took Mattawa right along with him. I remember talking to a woman in St. Petersberg, Florida during a

March break in 1971. When the woman found out that I was from Mattawa she pulled out a well worn copy of Ebony magazine with Dr. Monestime's picture on the cover. To her he was a champion of civil rights and she saw our little town as one of the most progressive places in the world."

Many letters of congratulations were received at the event including one from MP Mauril Belanger. (see sidebar above)

New Mattawa Hospital

The town of Mattawa proudly opened its new 20 million dollar hospital in October 2008.

The opening had many guests who played a part in the project. Minister of Tourism Monique Smith and Minister of Energy and Infrastructure George Smitherman represented the provincial government. MP Anthony Rota represented the Federal government. Mattawa Mayor Dean Backer and mayors from the surrounding area joined hospital staff, their Board, other key players and the people of the Mattawa area.

The Monestime connection to Mattawa healthcare was recognized when Vala Monestime Belter was given the honour of acting as Master of Ceremonies

Right: The new Mattawa Hospital. Below: The ribbon cutting at the opening of the hospital. Vala Monestime Belter is on the far left. (BE)

of the opening and was piped in with other dignitaries for the ribbon cutting. Several Sisters of Charity nurses from Ottawa told Vala how the Sisters remembered and admired her father from when they worked with him in Ottawa, Mattawa and Quebec City.

A 24 page supplement of the *North Bay Nugget* provided an opportunity for the many people involved in the project to be recognized and to pass on their congratulations.

Vala Monestime Belter noted that her "dad would be proud of the people of Mattawa because they continued to fight for a modern hospital for the town."

With the new hospital and the Algonquin Nursing Home the people of Mattawa receive state of the art service.

Dr. Monestime's Recognition on Mattawa's 125 Anniversary and the Centenary of his birth.

The Monestime family has announced it is donating land next to the nursing home to build 12 apartments for seniors supportive housing as a thank you to Mattawa and to celebrate their father's 100th birthday.

As this book was being prepared it was announced that the Mattawa Council Chamber will be renamed the Dr. S. F. Monestime Council Chamber. The mounting of a portrait of Dr. Monestime and a plaque will be part of this event.

Current Algonquin Nursing Home Administrator Vala Monestime Belter (left) and Director of Care Janet McNabb in the ANH office. Portraits of ANH founders Zena and Firmin Monestime are on the wall behind them.

WHERE RIVERS MEET

Summary & Conclusion

There are many tributaries in the river of life, and many stories where rivers meet. This is one of those stories, one that honours the Canadian multicultural mix that is so much a part of our culture. The Monestime story is a model of the success of strong family solidarity, hard work, integrity and a supporting community.

This book is a chronological history of the Monestime family from their places of birth to the present day. In the case of Dr. Monestime, it covers his life from his Haitian birth on December 16, 1909 through 100 years including his children and grandchildren, to the present day.

This book is the story of a man, who was a doctor for forty years, including successful careers in Haiti and Canada, two long periods of medical training, thousands of operations as a surgeon, and many births as a doctor; he could be remembered for this alone.

But the story is much more than that, when you add his widely recognized remarkable political career as Canada's, if not North America's, first Black mayor. The legacy of his achievements for the people of Mattawa and beyond has made him something of a legend.

The Algonquin Nursing Home, which he and his wife Zena worked so hard to establish, is a living monument to them. It is important to note that this is not just a story about Dr. Monestime, but it is also the story of the equally powerful achievement of his wife Zena and daughter Vala in making the Algonquin Nursing Home what it is today. The long-term care of the hundreds of Mattawa and area elderly with Zena working into her 80s and Vala currently administering the facility, extends the legend.

The other obviously significant part of this story is that none of this could have happened without the support of the people of Mattawa who encouraged, supported and accepted the Monestimes into their community—Where Rivers Meet.

Jubilant over her husband's victory, Mrs. S. F. Monestime congratulates her husband, who was re-elected mayor of Mattawa on Monday. Dr. Monestime defeated his only opponent by exactly 400 votes. —Photo by Len Selle

Appendix 1. Haitian History

The current Republic of Haiti shares the Caribbean island of Hispaniola with the Dominican Republic. Shaped like a "giant lobster claw" Haiti is a mountainous nation that occupies the western third of the Island. It is a colourful country with blue skies, brilliant flowers, white beaches and green farmlands that back against the mountains.

The Island of Hispanola had a population of three million Taino people when Christopher Columbus arrived in 1492. Spanish entrepreneurs seeking gold enslaved the Taino people and they eventually died off through disease, over work or death trying to escape. In a few decades the Spanish brought in African slaves to work in the mines and plantations.

In 1625 the French landed on the island, fought for control and eventually won the western third of the island which became Saint-Domingue. The French developed plantations of cotton, sugar cane and coffee. They brought in their own slaves by the thousands. When the French Revolution broke out in France in 1789 there were some 45,000 slaves and 30,000 free people of mixed blood in Saint-Domingue .

A Haitian revolution took place shortly after the one in France. With the colony facing a full-scale invasion by Britain, the rebel slaves emerged as a powerful military force, under the leadership of Toussaint Louverture, Jean-Jacques Dessalines, and Henri Christophe. Louverture successfully drove back the British and by 1798 was the de facto ruler of the colony.

In 1804 Jean-Jacques Dessalines declared independence, reclaiming the indigenous Taíno name of Haiti (Land of Mountains) for the new nation. Haiti is the world's oldest Black republic and the second-oldest republic in the Western Hemisphere, after the United States.

By 1874, after a period of instability, Haiti enjoyed a relatively stable period with peaceful transitions of government and a flowering of art and culture. This period of relative stability and prosperity ended in 1911 when revolution broke out and the country slid once again into disorder and debt. In 1915 the United States, which had banking interests in Haiti and feared a growing German influence, occupied the country. They stayed until 1934 while keeping a financial interest until mid-century.

Haitians resented the Americans and resisted them. One of their national heroes is General Charlemagne Peralte who was killed in 1919 by the occupying forces. Thousands of Haitians died during the occupation with some estimations as high as 15,000. In 1930, Sténio Vincent, a long-time critic of the occupation, was elected President, and the U.S. began to withdraw its forces.

It was during this time that Dr. Monestime was growing up in Haiti. He became involved in the Government first under President Vincent and then under the President Élie Lescot in 1941. After Dr. Monestime left in 1946, a military junta handed over power to Dumarsais Estimé, a black Haitian, who introduced major reforms in labor and social policy, and greatly expanded civil and political liberties for the Black majority. Another coup brought to power General Paul Magloire in 1950 who established a dictatorship which lasted until December 1956, when he was forced to resign as a result of a general strike. After a period of disorder Dr. François Duvalier, coincidentally a former school mate of Dr. Monestime's, was elected President

Sténio Vincent

Élie Lescot

General Paul Magloire

in September 1957.

Over the next 30 years Duvalier and his son "Baby Doc" ruled by force. A small group at the top lived the good life while the ordinary citizen lived in poverty. Many left the country to settle elsewhere.

"Baby Doc" was finally expelled in 1986 and a new constitution provided for free elections. Reverend Jean-Bertrand Aristide was elected in 1990 but was overthrown within a year and anarchy reigned until the U.S. again brought in troops and Aristide returned and won another election. International troops provided peace keeping. Aristede again left under strange circumstance. Another election took place in 2006 with Rene Paval winning a five year term.

Haitians in Canada

The large Haitian population and their difficult way of life has led to many leaving for other countries for a better opportunity. In the 1940s the few Haitian immigrants to Canada were usually professionals. Even then indications are that there were less than 40 arrivals. Dr. Monestime was one.

In the late 1950s during the Duvalier era and to the present day thousands sought hope in the United States and Canada and elsewhere. It is estimated that there are over one million Haitians in the U.S. - many in the New York and Miami areas and other cities where Haitian cultural "enclaves" have developed.

Many came to Florida illegally in makeshift boats.

Many Haitian immigrants chose Quebec as their new home because of the language and religion. About 95% of all Canadian arrivals of Haitians overall went to Quebec. Since professionals were not allowed to leave Haiti, many came as political refugees without proper documents and were welcomed.

Many who came later were sponsored immigrants who were accepted because they had relatives here. Most live in and around Montreal. Michaëlle Jean came to Canada in 1968. She became Canada's first Black Governor General in 2008.

There is extensive Haitian cultural activity in Canada. They have their own newspapers, periodicals and radio programs. There is an excellent Haitian art scene with paintings, sculpture and music. There are many outstanding authors and athletes, especially in Quebec.

Many Haitians have aligned with other Blacks for political and social reasons to fight some of the contradictions and barriers in society here as elsewhere. There is no doubt that Haitians are a vibrant community with a major role to play in Canada's multicultural society.

Haiti Today

Haiti is the most densely populated nation (over 8 million people) and the poorest in the western hemisphere. About 80% live under the poverty line and 54% live in abject poverty. Most Haitians work in the agricultural sector on small subsistence farms. Deforestation and weather continue to create great difficulty.

There is some sugar refining, flour milling, textiles, and product assembly based on imported components. Haitians depend on imports for much of their food, manufactured goods, machinery, transportation equipment, fuel, and raw materials. Most comes from the U.S. Canada provides millions in aid, peacekeepers and other support.

Life expectancy in Haiti is 51 years and literacy is about 50%. French and Creole are the languages of the country with French primarily used by the upper class. The country is primarily Roman Catholic with some Voodoo practiced. There is an approximate 10% professional population. About 95% of Haitians are of African origin.

Canada contributes millions in aid to Haiti. Canada's Governor General Michaëlle Jean visited Haiti in early 2009 where she met the new Haitian Prime Minister Michele Pierre-Louis whom she described as "very dynamic and worth knowing." Michaëlle Jean emphasized that Haiti was politically stable but that the situation was "terrible" because of the food crisis, the hurricanes and tropical storms in 2008, and that the situation was becoming worse with the economic crisis.

Appendix 2. Black History in Canada

There is currently a growing body of work adding to our understanding of Black history in Canada and in Ontario. It is beyond the scope of this book to profile all of these resources but some of interest follow. Excellent material is available on line. Do a search for "Ontario Black History" for a start.

Dr. Fred Landon the former Head of the library at the University of Western Ontario is considered "the most prolific writer on 19th century Ontario Black History." Bryan Walls was the first Black president of the Ontario Historical Society. My son and I had the pleasure of being awarded the Society's Fred Landon History Award by Dr. Walls in 2000.

Dr. Walls was one of the speakers at a major conference called Forging Freedom in 2007 which celebrated the bicentennial of the abolition of the Atlantic slave trade in 1807. The event was co-sponsored by the Ontario Historical Society and the Ontario Black History Society .

Dr. Walls is a fifth generation Black from Windsor where his family has preserved their old homestead as an historic site and Underground Railway Museum. Bryan's father fought a long and successful battle to become the first Black member of the Essex County Golf Club. Bryan Walls wrote a well received book *The Road* that *Led to Somewhere* in 1980 about Earl Walls, a member of the Boxing Hall of Fame.

The Ontario Black History Society (OBHS) is a non-profit charity dedicated to the study, preservation and promotion of Black history and heritage through education, research and cooperation. They have a special interest in the inclusion of Black history in the school curriculum. They are also a driving force behind Black History Month each February starting in 1996. They are an excellent resource. Their office in Toronto is aligned with the Ontario Heritage Foundation which recognizes various Black History sites and among other things provides plaques locating important historical locations.

There are several lists of Black firsts of various lengths and Dr. Monestime is usually included as the first Black mayor in Canada. This list of firsts includes Leonard Braithwaite the first Black member of the Ontario Legislature (1963). Rosemary Brown the first Black B.C. Member of Parliament (1972). Lincoln Alexander the first Black Federal Member of Parliament and cabinet minister (1979). He was Ontario's Lieutenant Governor from 1985 to 1991. Michaëlle Jean, who emigrated to Canada from Haiti in 1968, became the first Black Governor General (2008).

Looking at the wider picture, the remarkable victory of Barak Obama in 2008 to the most prestigious political role in the world is a watershed moment. He did it on the 45th anniversary of Dr. Martin Luther King Jr.'s famous "I have a dream" speech at the Lincoln Memorial in Washington D.C.

Dr. Daniel Hill who came to Canada about the same time as Dr. Monestime came to Mattawa had a remarkable career. Dr. Hill became Director of the Ontario Human Rights Commission, the first government agency protecting citizens from discrimination and was Ontario Ombudsman for five years. He wrote the book *The Freedom*

Seekers: Blacks in Early Canada. His son Dan Hill is one of Canada's best known singers and songwriters and still makes his living writing. His brother Lawrence Hill is the author of *The Book of Negroes* (2008) and *Black Berry, Sweet Juice: On Being Black and White in Canada* (2001). The book provides an interesting look at Black history and what it means to be Black.

One of the best books on Black History up to 1971 is *The Blacks in Canada: A History* by Robin W. Winks, republished in 1996. He outlines the various waves of Blacks coming to Canada as fugitive slaves, Loyalists, and those fleeing the American Revolution and the Civil War. Dr. Monestime is briefly mentioned in the book. Numerous books about the history of various locations where Blacks settled in Ontario have been written and are being written and there are numerous Museums and Heritage sites. I have mentioned some of these in my Heritage Perspectives column in the Community Voices newspaper. The 2006 Canadian Census report indicates that there are 662,000 Blacks in Canada with 78% in 5 cities. The census states there were 350 in North Bay. One of the North Bay

Blacks was Kwadino Adases, a student at Nipissing University who founded the Nipissing University African Canadian Club to enhance knowledge of their experience. Anyone can attend.

In 2006 The *North Bay Nugget* reported on the work of Antonio Fernandes, a Black refugee from Angola, who was adopted in North Bay and attends Scollard Hall. He and his classmates wanted to celebrate Black History Month so they brought guest speaker, Minnijean Brown Trickey, a friend of Antonio's mother. Minnijean is a Canadian Black student who attended a white university in the US after the U.S. Supreme Court ruled that segregation was illegal. She also went to school in Sudbury and Ottawa. She worked for U.S. President Bill Clinton on diversity issues. The Nugget story listed a few well known Blacks including Dr. Monestime.

Karolyn Smardz Frost, the Director of the Ontario Historical Society, won the Governor General's Award for her book *I've Got a Home in Glory Land* in 2007. Lawrence Hill's novel *The Book of Negroes* was a multi award winning book in 2008. In 2009 it won the CBC's Canada Reads competition.

 A few places to visit on the web:

Haiti and Haitian History:

1. A detailed history of Haiti-**www.travelinghaiti.com/history.asp**
2. The Wikipedia site-**www.en.wikipedia.org/wiki/History_of_Haiti**

Black History in Canada:

1. Ontario Black History Society- **www.blackhistorysociety.ca**
2. Multicultural Canada-**www.multiculturalcanada.ca/Encyclopedia/A-Z/a16**
3. Historica's Black History Canada site-**www.blackhistorycanada.ca/**
4. Da Costa 400: A Celebration of 400 Years Black Canadian Heritage-**www.dacosta400.ca**
5. Wikipedia's list of famous Black Canadians-**www.en.wikipedia.org/wiki/List_of_Black_Canadians**

Views expressed on the above websites do not necessarily reflect the views of the producers of this book.

Appendix 3. Dr. Martin Luther King Jr. 1963

In 1963 the same year Dr. Monestime won the election to become the Mayor of Mattawa famous civil rights leader Dr. Martin Luther King Jr. was jailed in Birmingham Alabama for participating in a non-violent demonstration against rampant segregation in the United States. Eight white religious leaders criticized King for his presence in Birmingham and told him he should wait and be patient for change. Dr. King wrote a long letter in longhand in his jail cell to the clergymen making his position clear. A few quotations from the letter show the contrast with Mattawa the same year.

Dr. King wrote: "We know through painful experience that freedom is never voluntarily given by the oppressor; it must be demanded by the oppressed. Frankly, I have never yet engaged in a direct-action movement that was 'well timed' according to the timetable of those who have not suffered unduly from the disease of segregation. For years now I have heard the word 'wait.' It rings in the ear of every negro with a piercing familiarity. This 'wait' has almost always meant 'never.'

We must come to see with the distinguished jurist of yesterday that 'justice too long delayed is justice denied.' We have waited for more than three hundred and forty years for our God-given and constitutional rights."

Further along in the letter he wrote: "I guess it is easy for those who have never felt the stinging darts of segregation to say 'wait.' But when you have seen vicious mobs lynch your mothers and fathers at will and drown your sisters and brothers at whim; when you have seen hate-filled policemen curse, kick, brutalize, and even kill your Black brothers and sisters with impunity; when you see the vast

Dr. Martin Luther King Jr.

majority of your twenty million negro brothers smothering in an airtight cage of poverty in the midst of an affluent society; when you suddenly find you tongue twisted and your speech stammering as you seek to explain to your six-year-old daughter why she cannot go to the public amusement park that has just been advertised on television, and see tears welling up in her little eyes when she is told that Funtown is closed to colored children, and see the depressing clouds of inferiority begin to form in her little mental sky, and see her begin to distort her little personality by unconsciously developing a bitterness toward white people; when you have to concoct an answer for a five-year-old son asking in agonizing pathos, 'Daddy, why do white people treat colored people so mean?'; when you take a cross-country drive and find it necessary to sleep night after night in the uncomfortable corners of your automobile because no motel will accept you; when you are humiliated day in and day out by nagging signs reading 'white' and 'colored;' when your first

name becomes 'nigger' and your middle name becomes 'boy' (however old you are) and your last name becomes 'John,' and when you are harried by day and haunted by night by the fact that you are a Negro, living constantly at tiptoe stance, never quite knowing what to expect next, and plagued with inner fears and outer resentments; when you are forever fighting a degenerating sense of 'nobodyness' - then you will understand why we find it difficult to wait. There comes a time when the cup of endurance runs over and men are no longer willing to be plunged into an abyss of injustice where they experience the bleakness of corroding despair. I hope, sirs, you can understand our legitimate and unavoidable impatience."

King also made his famous "I have a dream" speech on the steps of the Lincoln Memorial in Washington D.C. and was named "Man of the Year" by Time Magazine the same year as the letter above.

In 1968 the year he was assassinated at age 39 Dr. King became the youngest man to win the Nobel Peace Prize. Martin Luther King Day was established in 1983. In a Gallup Poll King was recognized as the second most admired American of the 20th century and a Discovery Channel contest found him to be "The Greatest American of all Time."

It is interesting that 45 years later almost to the day Barak Obama became the first Black president of the United States and in 2009 was inaugurated the day after Martin Luther King Day. Coincidentally, it is interesting that forty five years after he was elected the first Black mayor in Canada Dr. Monestime is being recognized in Mattawa on the centenary of his birth.

Appendix 4. Mattawa Poet Len G. Selle

The title of this book *Where Rivers Meet* comes from the first line of a poem written by Len G. Selle. Len was an Ontario Hydro employee stationed in Mattawa in the 1950s & 60s. The Poem called *Mattawa* is reproduced in Leo Morel's book *The Meeting of the Waters* and elsewhere in various Mattawa publications. The sign at the western entrance to Mattawa contains the words "There is a story here" and below that "Where rivers meet." The poem - a sonnet, resonates with the experience Dr. Monestime had. The poem is on page 3.

Mr. Selle wrote many other poems, many of which appear in two books of his work. (The North Bay Public Library and the John Dixon Library in Mattawa have copies).

One of the books has an introduction by former Mattawa English teacher W. J. Dixon whose name is remembered as a leader in developing Mattawa's John Dixon Library which is named after him.

The following poem *Home for the Aged* was written long before the Algonquin Nursing Home opened but is an interesting example of his work. The poem follows.

Home for the Aged
They who live here are older than these walls,
Their faces deeper scarred than brick or stone,
Along the corridors and silent halls
Eternal mothers walk their ways alone.
From rocking chairs their whispered voices float
Like reeded pipes in some old pastoral scene;
Fragments of dreams spill from each wrinkled throat,
Dead tales of things that were, or might have been.

Outside, the old men sitting in the sun
Nod pleasantly above their knobby canes;
Old wars are fought, old victories rewon,
Manhood achievements storm their hoary brains . . .
Home for the aged - harbour of ancient ships -
For you the storms are past, the soft winds blow;
You with your shaking heads, your trembling lips,
And beauty such as youth can never know.

An effort was made to find further information on Mr Selle but nothing was forthcoming. We did find that he had many poems and articles published in newspapers including the North Bay Nugget. We noticed Mr. Selle's name as the photographer in the photo of Dr. Monestime and his wife Zena (Shown on page 73.) after Dr. Monestime's resounding re-election as Mayor in 1964.

Appendix 5. Mattawa History References

For further information on Mattawa history check the website www.vintagepostcards.org and under Nipissing History click on Mattawa. If you click on the photos they will enlarge.

Another source of information is a book by Leo Morel called *Mattawa: The Meeting of the Waters* published in 1980 but now out of print. Copies are available in libraries or by inter library loan, and at the Mattawa Museum.

Mattawa writer Gerry Therrien wrote a book called *Mattawa Our Timeless Town* in 2000. Copies are available through Gerry, or at the Mattawa Museum and in Libraries. There is a chapter on Dr. Monestime in the book. The Mattawa Museum on Explorers Point has an excellent range of displays and information on Mattawa including a Russian exhibit and one on Dr. Monestime. Check on their website at www.mattawmuseum.com for dates and times they are open.

Doug Mackey in his Heritage Perspectives column in the North Bay Nugget's Regional Supplement Community Voices has written many articles on Mattawa and area. Check his website www.pastforward.ca/perspectives and click on the column titles indicated below for a full and printable view of the column.

June 2, 2000	Mattawa's Roots Buried in History
June 9, 2000	Mattawa Area Holds Many Heritage Opportunities
June 16, 2000	Mattawa Woman (Gertrude Bernard) Grey Owl's Inspiration

Author

Doug Mackey: Doug is a former teacher, principal and school superintendent and now lives in Chisholm Township near North Bay, Ontario. As a former museum curator and as a regional historian Doug has written a weekly Heritage Perspectives column for the North Bay Nugget's Community Voices newspaper since 2000. (see www.pastforward.ca/perspectives)

Designer & Editor

Paul Mackey: Paul is a graphic designer, photographer and editor. He has designed and produced all of Past Forward's books and CDs.

Together Doug and his son Paul are **Past Forward Heritage Limited** a historical research, writing and publishing business.